The Challenge *to* Establishing *the* Imperishable Truth

IRH Press

Originally published in Japan
as *Fumetsu naru Mono eno Chosen
- Reisei no Jidai wo Hiraku tameni*
by IRH Press Co., Ltd., in December 2025.

IRH PRESS
New York

ISBN: 978-1-958655-39-9

Printed in Japan

First Edition

The Challenge *to* Establishing *the* Imperishable Truth

EL CANTARE

Ryuho Okawa

Now Is the Age of Spiritual Awakening

IRH Press

Contents

CHAPTER ONE

The Correct Understanding of the Afterlife

—Lecture on *A Life that Will Not Leave You in Trouble after Death*

CHAPTER TWO

The Ideal Education for Pursuing the Truth

—Lecture on *Spirituality and Education*

CHAPTER THREE

Why Is It a Problem to Live a Self-Centered Life?

—The Essential Mindset to Get Out of Unhappiness

CHAPTER FOUR

The Challenge to Establishing the Imperishable Truth

—Polish Your Mind Fully and Illuminate the World

CHAPTER FIVE

Awaken to the Value of Your Mind

—Light the Flame of Love in Each and Every Person

CHAPTER ONE

The Correct Understanding of the Afterlife

—Lecture on *A Life that Will Not Leave You in Trouble after Death*

Recorded in Japanese on October 3, 2010
at Happy Science Aomori Local Temple in Aomori, Japan.
English translation.

1

Why I Teach People How to Live a Life that Will Not Cause Them Trouble after Death

Hello, everyone in Aomori Local Temple and those in the Tohoku region who are watching this lecture via satellite broadcast. I visited Hachinohe Branch last year (2009), so I have now come to Aomori Prefecture two years in a row. Recently, I published a book (*Shinde-kara-Komaranai-Ikikata*, or literally, "A Life that Will Not Leave You in Trouble after Death"), which includes a lecture I gave at Hachinohe Branch (Jigoku-kara-no-Dasshutsu, or literally, "Getting Out of Hell" on September 22, 2009). It seems like the Tohoku region makes me want to preach afterlife-related topics.

On my way here, I saw the wharf and the ocean. [*To the audience at the main venue*] So, is that the well-known Tsugaru Strait? It's been my dream place. At last, I've seen it. It's famous for the song that goes [*sings*], "Getting off the night train that departed from Ueno Station, I saw the snow covering Aomori Station (from the lyrics of the song, "Tsugaru-Kaikyo Fuyu-geshiki," or literally, "Tsugaru Strait—Winter Scene," written by Yu Aku)," isn't it? [*Audience applauds*]

I saw it for the first time, although I should have seen it in the snow [*audience laughs*]. Unfortunately, it was not snowing but only drizzling. Anyway, I guessed right that it was the Tsugaru Strait. I now understand how it feels to be there. According to the internal reports I have received, Aomori Local Temple is closer to the ocean than Hachinohe Branch, which is why people are more open and cheerful here. Even so, I felt from looking at the scenery that people seemed to be rather affected by the gloomy mood of the song.

I am also slightly anxious. Honestly speaking, are my books too difficult for you? I'm a bit afraid that they are. This book (*Shinde-kara-Komaranai-Ikikata*) is relatively easy, so I think you can understand it, but what about my other books? I hope you at least have bookstores around here [*audience laughs*]. Of course, you do, which is good. I'm afraid and a bit worried that my books do not really satisfy your needs. But this is one of the easiest of my books to read. It compiles the lectures I gave in Iwate Prefecture, Aomori Prefecture, and Toyama Prefecture last September—about a year ago. So, I do not think it is too far from serving your needs.

The Tohoku region is, indeed, a very difficult place for me to give a lecture because every time I come here, I sense that it is difficult to get my message across. The atmosphere in this prayer hall is very light and bright, which relieves me, but otherwise, I imagine you are having a tough time every day living in the harsh environment. Aomori Prefecture, in particular, "competes" with Akita Prefecture in terms of the number of suicides. It is as though they are rivals competing for the top record in Japan. Except for the occasional times when Yamanashi Prefecture steals the top position, they are almost always near the top of the rankings and appear to be in competition with each other like two preparatory schools that have been built side-by-side.

I guess people tend to become depressed or gloomy when they live in a harsh environment with heavy snow. As I watched the scenery, I thought about various things and thought that the locals would certainly have no answer to the question, "How do you think you can make this town wealthier and more prosperous?" I would suggest that you turn defiant and start a new industry involving *itako* (female shaman), since itako used to be very popular around here. Of course, I'm saying this half-jokingly. Just the other day, I saw an event involving itako being held in front of a station around Sendai, and they were charging ¥4,000 (about US$27) per person for a session. I saw how itako are being "exported" there.

I believe Tohoku is one of the few regions in Japan where people tend to believe in the other world rather easily. But even though they easily come to believe in the other world, they are also more likely to commit suicide. So, it is an awkward place.

The major reason people suddenly decide to commit suicide might be that, unlike Christianity, Buddhism does not clearly teach that you cannot go to heaven if you commit suicide. Christianity teaches that people who commit suicide cannot enter heaven. Some churches even refuse to bury the bodies of those who killed themselves because they disobeyed God's Law. So, Christians face the risk of not being able to have their funerals conducted if they commit suicide.

In Japan, on the other hand, people are more familiar with the Buddhist teachings of the "impermanence of all things" and the "egolessness of all phenomena," so they probably think that it is not good to be attached to life in this world after they die, and therefore take their physical lives more lightly. If this is what they think, I must supplement my teachings (that I taught as Shakyamuni Buddha), which is why I published the book. I believe there is a need for me to teach people how they should live in a way that will not cause them trouble after death.

2

It Is Wrong to Think that Everything Ends with Death

You will suffer ten times more in the afterlife if you commit suicide

It is probably the case that many people commit suicide because their lives are full of suffering and they have a hard time living in this world. But unfortunately, I must say that it is a mistake to think that everything ends with death or that you will be freed from your suffering when you die.

I have been conducting religious activities for 30 years now. During this time, I have gained a lot of knowledge about the Spirit World, and this year in particular, I have published many spiritual messages. The total number of my books has exceeded 600 (at the time of the lecture; as of December 2025, more than 3,250 books have been published). I have spent years trying to prove the existence of the other world. So, from the perspective of someone like me, it is clearly wrong to deny the existence of the other world or the Spirit World and think, "Life in this world is full of suffering, but I can be happy or at least be freed from suffering by taking my life." This is the first point I want to make.

Many people do not know what happens after death because no one has ever taught them about it. That is why they can only think about escaping from their current suffering through suicide. But the truth is that the happiness and sadness of this world will be amplified tenfold in the other world. You will feel ten times more happiness or ten times more sadness. Please know that the other world is like this.

Therefore, people who led a happy life—a life that would be blessed by God or Buddha—will be able to experience happiness ten times greater than what they felt in this world when they return to the other world. On the other hand, people whose suffering and sadness seemed like the world of hell when they lived in this world will feel more real and substantial suffering and sadness in the other world. So, people who die with these kinds of emotions will experience even greater suffering and sadness after they die. They may have thought that they could escape from their suffering and sadness by taking their own lives, but in reality, the opposite situation will unfold; their suffering will be amplified tenfold. You need to know this.

There are people who miraculously survive a suicide attempt and come back to this world. Most of these people tell of their experience of having glimpsed the so-called "world of hell" and often say that they do not want to attempt suicide again. It seems like most of them saw a world that is far from pleasant. It is a world full of strange and scary things, a world too creepy to live in. So, many of them say that the world on earth is a much better place compared to the one they saw. They are indeed right. Many have experienced this.

Buddhism does not clearly teach about suicide. It is especially unclear because of the description of how Shakyamuni Buddha mercifully defended his disciples for having taken their lives. Some disciples went overboard with their ascetic training by starving themselves or taking their lives to get rid of their attachment to their physical bodies. To console their souls, Shakyamuni Buddha told them that they had removed all their attachments to this world. On the other hand, he also taught that one must not commit suicide. Both teachings have been handed down, so the Buddhist stance on suicide is a little uncertain.

However, I must clearly say now that people should not commit suicide. There is virtually nothing good that comes out of it.

Of course, this does not mean that everyone who commits suicide will suffer in hell for all eternity. Christianity teaches that those who commit suicide will forever be banished to hell because once you fall to hell, you can never get out of it. But in reality, those people do not stay in hell forever.

In the past, I have introduced some exceptional cases. For example, Takamori Saigo and General Maresuke Nogi fell on their own swords. They literally committed suicide. They followed the customs of the times and killed themselves to finish their lives as a true samurai. I doubt that they went straight back to heaven after death; they probably spent some time in hell suffering. But after spending a certain period in hell, they both returned to their rightful places in heaven. They had very pure hearts and were admired by many people when they lived, so this worked as tremendous "buoyancy" for them to return to heaven. Many people respected and admired them and wished for them to return to their original place in heaven, the world of gods. Those thoughts worked to lift them out of hell and helped them return to heaven rather quickly. They held the right view of life and death and believed in the existence of the other world. What is more, they chose to take their lives because they felt responsible for what had happened in the third-dimensional world. So, there are slightly different aspects to their cases.

There are some exceptions, but in general, people who commit suicide will find themselves in a harsh situation after death.

You are being tested to see what you can accomplish in the 30,000 days of your life

There are certainly various reasons why people commit suicide. Some people take their own lives because they want to escape from the illness they suffer. When people get older, they often suffer from diseases, so they may wish to ease that suffering. But there are people who choose to kill themselves not for their own desire to be free from suffering but to lighten the burden on their family members. For example, they may feel bad about being a continuous burden on their family and commit suicide because they want to reduce it. This is truly heartbreaking. Nowadays, there is even a term called "caregiving hell" where some people are stuck between a rock and a hard place. Especially when their children are still young and need a lot of care and attention, they develop what is called the "sandwich syndrome." This is a new English term that describes the suffering that comes from being caught between the task of taking care of both their children and their parents. In this situation, there are elderly people who decide to commit suicide because they do not want to trouble their family any longer. This is very sad.

A bad financial situation due to a recession can be another reason. Happy Science basically teaches the importance of self-help, but after coming here to the northernmost region of Honshu Island, I keenly feel that it would be very difficult to launch an industry here with the spirit of self-help alone. It would sound too cold to encourage you to do so. I have heard that the *shinkansen* (bullet train) will finally extend its route to Aomori in December, so I expect that your future will be a little brighter—or rather, much brighter. Perhaps, people will no longer sing the song I mentioned, "Tsugaru-Kaikyo Fuyu-geshiki," but having the shinkansen running here is, indeed, a blessing; it will certainly be more convenient for businesses here. As you can see, in some cases, you need national-level involvement to solve a financial issue.

In this world, there are various kinds of suffering, including a substandard life, but if you use it as a reason to say that you can only be happy if you leave this world, you are clearly mistaken. The basic teaching of Buddhism states that, as long as you live in this world, you cannot escape the Four Pains of Birth, Aging, Illness, and Death. There is also the pain of not getting what you want, which is very common and is one of the Eight Pains. But even though you live in a world like this, you also need to know that you do not just suffer for the sake of suffering. You are being tested to see what you can grasp as you go through harsh training of being in a physical body. No matter how long you live, you only have slightly over 30,000 days of life, so there is no need for you to commit suicide. Your life will eventually come to an end. What, then, will you accomplish in this 30,000-day life that you were given by God? How will you live it? These are the questions you must answer.

3

"Life after Death" Is 100 Percent Guaranteed to Exist

Why do I keep saying that the afterlife exists?

I guarantee you, 100 percent, that there is an afterlife or the world after death. So, please take my word and believe that it exists. I have been saying this for 30 years, so please just accept it and don't be picky about the small details. Simply believe by telling yourself, "Ryuho Okawa is saying this. Why not just believe it? It's too much of a hassle to argue anyway." There is no way you can explore the afterlife yourself, so just believe in someone who has been continually exploring it, talking about it consistently, and publishing books and giving lectures on it. This year alone, I have already given over 190 lectures and am aiming to give my 200th lecture in October (at the time of the lecture). I would not be able to keep doing this based on lies—there is no way I would have been able to continue teaching about it if it wasn't true.

Many people in this world are living based on wrong values without ever doubting them. This is inviting unhappiness into their lives, so we need to help them change the way they think. That is why I continue to teach about the true worldview and about true values. I have taught these things across Japan, and now, my teachings have spread overseas as well. My teachings are universal.

Currently, no one else in the world is teaching about the other world as clearly as I am. I am the only one. No other person can speak about the Spirit World, or the other world, so clearly and thoroughly. I am traveling around the world to teach the Truth not as a "living fossil (*kaseki*)" but as a "living miracle (*kiseki*)." Today, I have come to Aomori, which is home to various legends, such as the story of Jesus Christ coming here from across the seas or of the Buddhist monk Kukai coming here. But while these might be legends, it is a fact that Ryuho Okawa came here. It is a fact. A man, who has a complete understanding of the Truth about the other world and this world, came to Aomori and spoke in front of people—this fact will remain in history. I hope you will deeply understand the value of this.

I am an expert on the other world; I know everything about it, including its front and rear sides. I know the personalities of various spirits in the other world, as well as their spirit types, thoughts, and approaches. I know everything about angels and devils, too, including what they are thinking, doing, feeling, or aiming to do, and what they think about humans. I know everything. A person of this stature is now standing here in front of you.

My opinions on Japanese education and mass media

I have been traveling around the world to teach people the Truth. While it is very difficult to gain an understanding from Japanese society as a whole, people in countries that are open to religious Truth are more willing to accept my teachings, regardless of their nationality. My teachings are spreading more widely in those countries. For example, Brazil is a very spiritual place, and so is India. We are currently planning to build a Happy Science temple in Bodhgaya, India, which is the center and origin of Buddhism. My teachings are spreading widely in India, especially in Mumbai—formerly known as Bombay—where a TV station aired my lectures over the course of six weeks and is planning to air a Happy Science movie in the seventh week as the finale (at the time of the lecture). This shows how widely my teachings have spread there. The local members are working hard, and I am apparently "lecturing in Hindi" without knowing. I am not sure if they used subtitles or dubbed over my voice, but anyway, apparently, my lectures come with Hindi translation. Happy Science is spreading in many countries, including more new branches in Africa, as well. This shows that the Truth is universal. I want everyone to know this.

Despite this, Japan is still stubbornly resisting accepting the Truth. The Japanese education system and mass media never touch upon the other world or the soul, nor are they willing to accept it. Medicine does not touch upon the subject of the soul, either. They just conclude that the soul is the result of the functions of the nervous system or the brain. They rule out the possibility of the existence of the soul, without even considering a 50-50 chance of it being true. They have given up on exploring it.

The same is true with education. Decades ago, school education started with teaching kids about the age of the gods, but now, teachers think that it is embarrassing to talk about stories like that. So, instead, they talk about the idea of how some clumps of protein started to move, evolved into animals, and eventually became humans, or an absurd story like how lizards that used to crawl on the Galapagos Islands somehow developed into humans over the years. But I want to tell those teachers, "Enough is enough!" They might as well "interview" the lizards living today and ask them why they are still lizards and not humans. Teachers could ask, "It's better to be human, so why haven't you become a human already? Why are you choosing to remain a lizard forever?" But the truth is that a lizard is a lizard and a snake is a snake. There are no creatures that are "in transition" in our world now. Every species exists in its complete form. There is not a single creature that is in the process of becoming human. All of them are complete as they are. Each creature exists in its complete form.

We need to think about why this is so. Why is every species in its complete form? The lizards on the Galapagos Islands are not lizards just because they happened to be born there. Even if you bring a lizard from the Galapagos to Japan, it will still be a lizard; it will not suddenly turn into a Japanese person and start walking around on two legs. You may wonder why, but it is what it is; lizards are lizards wherever they go. This shows that the various creatures are accepted as they are. We need to know this.

4
The Happiness of Being Born Human

It is truly a blessing to be a human

First and foremost, we must realize how much of a blessing it is to have been born human. It is wonderful to have the ability to understand things. It is a blessing, indeed.

My family used to own a rabbit. Our first rabbit lived for one and a half years before it died. Then, within a month, it was reborn elsewhere and has never (spiritually) shown up before me since then. Our second rabbit lived for about seven years. It was a rather "virtuous" rabbit and was even given its own room. The other day, I "met" this rabbit, or to be more specific, saw its spirit for the first time in a year after its death. But a rabbit is a rabbit even after it dies; it could not speak. It could not speak while it was alive, and it could not speak even after death. Animals that appear in the old Japanese tales can surely talk, be it a rabbit or a crane, but a real rabbit cannot talk even after a year has passed since it became a spirit. This made me realize how much of a blessing it is to be a human. A rabbit cannot speak, even as a spirit. I believe that the second rabbit was a virtuous one, but even so, it could not speak.

Again, being a human is truly a blessing. You can tell others what you are thinking. The basic emotions of joy, anger, sadness, and pleasure can create heaven and hell, but even though they can create hell, it is still a blessing to be able to feel such emotions, think about them, and express them. We need to know this happiness. I would like to tell you this today.

You may feel that you are lacking a countless number of things, but you need to realize how much you have already been given. Who, other than humans, could build the shinkansen to Aomori? Which animals could do so? Gorillas, elephants, or pandas? They are, indeed, physically stronger than humans, but they could not build the shinkansen. Humans can build it because they can plan, do the math, engineer, and support it financially. Humans were able to construct the shinkansen because they developed their civilization. We are living in an advanced society. By inventing the shinkansen, humans were finally able to "run faster" than a cheetah.

So, even though the world may appear to be full of suffering, humans are leading far better lives than animals. That is another way to look at it. You must know this. For example, you can understand my words because you have learned the standard form of Japanese partly through the NHK news, although you may notice that the standard

Japanese, Kansai, and Tokushima dialects are sometimes mixed in my lectures. This is also a blessing. It is even possible to translate what I say into English and other languages. Since you are a human, you can convey my message through a translation or an interpretation. The fact that you are a human being gives you an infinite number of blessings.

God's justice ultimately lies in the law of cause and effect

What I believe is most wonderful is that justice—a popular word nowadays—is always served. I believe that the ultimate form of God's justice lies in the law of cause and effect, otherwise known as causality. In the long run, the law of cause and effect unfailingly proves right on the individual level as well as on the global level.

I believe that
This law of cause and effect is justice itself.

Act rightly.
Think rightly.
Speak rightly.

Then, the right result will eventually and surely come to you.
The world is designed that way.
The two worlds,
This world and the other world,
Exist to complete the law of cause and effect.

In this world, a person past the age of 100 may die alone without anyone noticing, only to be discovered later as skeletal remains. However, if the person had lived a virtuous life, their spirit would surely have returned to heaven, not wandering around in this world as a lost spirit. This is true even if the dead body is found years later. People always reap an appropriate outcome.

Nothing can obscure the law of cause and effect. The kind of life you live will be judged fairly, and you will surely receive your own "report card of life." Those who worked hard despite the hardships of this world will definitely find the radiance of their effort turn into virtue and adorn their souls. Your effort will make your soul shine; it will definitely shed light.

In general, there is a rough plan for each person's life, and everyone has their own life span. Everyone will die one day. No one can escape death. Happy Science offers various ritual prayers to cure illnesses, and some people may be able to get over their illnesses for a time by taking ritual prayers. Miraculous healing may occur to those who still have a special mission to fulfill in this world. Even so, there is no doubt that everyone has to leave this world one day. However, this itself is a form of blessing. The changing of the guard leads to renewal of the world and makes way for the young. Seeing young people take a leading role in society is a form of happiness. Because of this, you could say that aging beautifully is also a very happy experience.

I, myself, am doing my best to resist aging and am always trying to stay young so that I do not get treated as "bulk waste" by my children. I always strive to make sure I do not give them the impression that I am getting old. Even so, the power of young people continues to grow and pushes us older generations out "above the clouds," day after day.

So, I continue to do what I must do. I have a map of Japan on the wall of my room, and I mark all the Happy Science local temples that have been built around the country. There is a white circle by the name of each local temple, such as Aomori Local Temple, and when I return from a lecture tour there, I find a cherry blossom sticker pasted on the circle [*gesturing pasting a sticker on the map with his right hand*]. There are many cherry blossoms blooming all over Japan, so the map has gotten much, much brighter. It is a little embarrassing to say this because it feels a bit childish, but it is a way I can leave a mark to show everywhere I go on a lecture tour. I do this, hoping to leave behind a record of where I visited and sowed the seeds of Buddha's Truth.

Everyone will eventually face the end of their life. But I really want you to know that this world and the other world exist and that the way you live in this world will be recorded on your "report card." It will determine what kind of life you will live in the other world. It also affects the kind of life you will plan for your next life, that is, the next time you are born into this world. These things are all connected. So, there is not a single bit of waste in what you do. Once you know this, you will certainly change the way you live.

Have the right faith and live to love others

• Take a firm hold of religious faith

If I were to narrow down the important attitudes to have when living in this world, I would state the following two points. One is to take a firm hold of religious faith. Whether you have religious faith or not is a major factor that determines which of two groups a person belongs to.

To be blunt, to have religious faith means you are not an animal. Animals do not have a clear sense of religious faith. Faith is something only humans can have. In other words, faith is the feeling of awe toward something invisible. This ability is unique to humans. Animals need things to be concrete to be able to feel something toward them. So, the ability to believe in the existence of something sacred, even if it cannot be seen or heard, is one of the powers humans possess to overcome their animalistic tendencies. Having this ability makes you very different from an animal. So, having faith is the first important attitude.

• Live with the wish to benefit others

The other important attitude comes down to the choice of whether you live a self-centered life or a life of altruism, in other words, a life of love for others. It depends on how much you can dedicate your life to the benefit of other people. If you have faith and you live with the wish to benefit other people, your life will never end in failure.

There are all kinds of earthly conditions in this world, but in reality, they are not what fundamentally determine the happiness of your life. If you count the number of things you are lacking or the things you do not have, there will be no end to them. It is impossible to have them all. But if you can hold onto the right faith and can live to love others, or live by loving others, that is all you need. You won't need anything else.

The unfavorable conditions that appear in your life are meant to test you. They are asking you, "Can you keep your faith in God despite this?" "Can you keep living for the sake of other people with this condition?" You may sometimes need to bear extra load. But it is nothing but a whetstone to polish your soul. It will make your soul shine even brighter.

Just look back at your Happy Science activities in this light. The atheistic and materialistic people who oppose you or people who are critical of religions are, of course, people you must guide, but they are also there to train you. They, themselves, have things to learn, but from your perspective, they got the short end of the stick and took the role of training you to make you tougher. When you go out to do missionary work, you may be rejected many times. People may refuse to take the book you are offering them. They may say, for example, "*A Life that Will Not Leave You in Trouble after Death*? What's good about this book? Just bring me a book that tells me how to win the lottery. I'm in trouble right now, so I don't care about the afterlife. Have Ryuho Okawa write the secrets to win millions in a lottery instead. Then, I will believe you." Others might ask you, "Well, it's nice that illnesses can be cured, but can't you make money fall from the sky?" "Can't you produce cash or a lump of gold?" "If you can make miracles happen, I would rather just ask you to make a block of gold or a diamond appear out of the blue." There are all kinds of people in this world, so you may be hurt by what they say. But please think that they are all there to make you stronger.

5

Change the Future with the Power of Buddha's Truth

It all started with my determination to spread the Truth

Every day, I regret that I am unable to spread the Truth as widely as I wish and the way I plan. But I repeatedly remind myself that, 30 years ago, I was doing this alone, and that 25 years ago, I did not yet have any organization (counting from the time of the lecture). Compared to those times, I have made significant progress, especially now that bookstores across Japan are selling my books, advertisements about my books are appearing, and I have become increasingly known overseas as well. Even though I myself have never been to countries like Uganda, Nigeria, and South Africa, many people, whom I have never met directly, have become believers of Happy Science and have conducted opening ceremonies for their new branches. I was deeply impressed when I watched their videos in the report*.

It all started with my determination to believe in the spiritual messages I received from the unseen world and to spread the Truth. Because of that resolve, the Truth has reached as far as the opposite side of the globe. People are working hard to do missionary work overseas despite many challenges. They go to new places to create new Happy Science believers so that there is at least one believer in every region. I am amazed by the effort they make despite the lack of tools and resources for missionary work.

Today, I read the local newspaper here in Aomori Prefecture and found an advertisement for my book, *A Life that Will Not Leave You in Trouble after Death*. The book was advertised in other newspapers as well, including Yomiuri Shimbun, Mainichi Shimbun, and Sankei Shimbun, taking up one-third of a page in each paper. I am grateful to them for advertising my books. I hope the bookstores around here have my books piled up like this [*pointing at the books stacked next to the podium*]. I am sure many people will buy them.

This is off topic, but I saw a Japanese tea ceremony gathering held at a hotel near here, where many women showed up in kimonos. When I walked into the entrance, I was mistaken for their tea master; everyone got excited, and some even came to greet me. Honestly, I was a little overwhelmed [*audience laughs*]. Because my books are advertised across Japan, people sometimes mistake me for someone else. Upon seeing the hotel manager coming to greet me at the door, the women in kimonos thought I was the tea master and gathered around me to greet me. It was a bit embarrassing.

I went off on a tangent, but anyway, I started my activities with no one else believing in me or standing by my side. Even so, my teachings have now spread widely, which makes me very happy. That being said, it is also true that we do not yet have enough power, so we want to summon all our strength to spread the Truth one step further.

I want Japanese members to be strong enough to support overseas missionary work

As I see how our members overseas are working hard to do missionary work in very difficult circumstances, I want us to build an even more solid foundation in Japan, which is the starting point of Happy Science missionary work, and help expand these missionary activities around the world. In fact, Happy Science has been spreading all around the world powerfully and strategically in order to become a world religion. This shows that our ambition is already transforming reality.

Even in China, which is currently a country with many problems, "undercover members" of Happy Science are working hard in secret to push forward with their missionary work. Despite the fear of being caught or arrested and put in prison, they are risking their lives to carry out this activity with a strong sense of mission. China used to be a great country of Buddhism and of Confucianism, so there is no way that the people there cannot understand Buddha's Truth. Chinese people can surely understand our teachings. The government now is forcing its people to believe in pro-government ideas that go against the Truth, but the Truth is flowing among people like underground water. So, Chinese people can definitely understand Buddha's Truth.

I want to change the future of the world with the power of Buddha's Truth. I strongly, strongly wish to do so. We do not have enough power yet. But within the next 10 years, I definitely want people in over 200 countries to acknowledge Happy Science and recognize that it has risen and has been carrying out activities all around the world in order to save the world. I am determined to push forward with our activities until people acknowledge and recognize us.

In this respect, I want you to understand the importance of keeping the torch of the Truth lit and continuing to spread this light in the northernmost region of Honshu, Japan. In the Tohoku region, transportation is not very convenient, and there may be other difficult conditions that allow you to make many excuses. However, the people in this area are honest and pure, so when faith takes root here, I am sure it will become very firm and strong. People living in the city tend to be fickle and are quick to change their minds. But if faith takes root in the Tohoku region, it will surely grow to be strong and resilient. So, I am hoping that all of you will make it happen.

All I wish is for everyone in this world and the other world to be happy

Let me summarize today's lecture simply.

I have revived the various teachings
Taught by religions in the past
In a new form that is most suitable for our time.
I am striving to save the world
By teaching people the Truth.
Please believe in these words of mine
And spread them.
I want everyone—
Both in this world and the other world—
To be as happy as they possibly can.
This is all I wish for.
To achieve this goal,
I want to establish a true religion
In the modern world
And show how religions should essentially be.

The mass media, which plays a big part in controlling Japan, believe that it is not good to advertise a religion. But as long as they have this as their ethics, we are still losing to them. We need to push our opinions forward strongly and change the mass media and their ethics so that one day they will say, "We need to spread the correct religious views all over Japan in order to make it a sound nation," or "We need to spread religious ideas to help people to get back on their feet, correct our school education, and improve our society." Although city people may view our activities lightly, I sincerely ask all of you to firmly plant the roots of your faith and establish strong faith in this northern region of Japan.

[Editor's note]

Later, in 2012, Okawa went to Uganda to give a lecture.

CHAPTER TWO

The Ideal Education for Pursuing the Truth

—Lecture on *Spirituality and Education*

Recorded in Japanese on August 8, 2010
at Happy Science Kumagaya Local Temple in Saitama, Japan.
English translation.

1
Spirituality-Based Education Versus Materialism-Based Education

Spiritual experiences I had during my late elementary school years

Hello everyone in the Kumagaya Local Temple, and everyone watching this lecture in other branches of Saitama Prefecture through satellite broadcasting. Today is August 8th. The cicadas are breaking a sweat and chirping loudly in this heat.

Kumagaya City is known for being one of the hottest cities in Japan, along with Tajimi City in Gifu Prefecture, so I was rather excited to experience the blazing heat. Unfortunately, the temperature today is only about 35°C (95°F), so I am a little disappointed [*audience laughs*]. When I visited Tajimi City in July, it was 38°C (100°F), and I acted tough and told everyone, "The people in India are celebrating Goseitansai (Celebration of the Lord's Descent) in 48°C (118°F), so we are still 10 degrees shy of that." But to tell the truth, I'm glad that you held the temperature to 35°C today. Thank you very much. Perhaps the cloudy weather helped lower the temperature.

When I arrived in Kumagaya, I saw some outdoor mist cooling systems installed in front of the station, so I sensed that this city must be rather wealthy. It makes sense to have systems like that installed in places that make large profits, such as Disneyland, but for other places, they are too costly. Usually, cities do not take any measures like this and rather let their citizens bear the heat, but this city has installed these systems. This is the first time I have seen a mist shower at a train station. It is quite impressive. I am not sure, but it may be that the city is making a lot of revenue off people's taxes.

Today's lecture is about my book, *Reisei-to-Kyoiku* (literally, "Spirituality and Education"). It comprises spiritual message sessions from Jean-Jacques Rousseau, Immanuel Kant, and Rudolf Steiner, all of which I conducted in an open session. I am supposed to give a lecture on this book, but I heard that there are about 50 non-Happy Science members listening to my lecture today. These people may find some of the words I use (such as the terminologies of Buddha's Truth) a little unfamiliar. I will keep the non-members in mind as I speak, but if there are some things you do not understand, please do not be concerned about them. I will be speaking in Japanese, so you will understand about 90 percent of what I say. Even if you do not grasp the other 10 percent, you should still be able to understand the general points of my talk, so please do not worry. Just to be clear, I have no intention of explaining all the details of this book (*Spirituality and Education*). Instead, I will be explaining in my own words what I think is the essence of education.

I believe I was in fifth grade in elementary school when I first came across the theme of spirituality and education. In those days, I would study and sleep in our secondary house, which was located about 660 feet from our main house (in Tokushima Prefecture). The secondary house was an old factory that my father used to run when he was younger, which later closed down. I would walk over to the building at night with my workbooks and stationery to study, and I would sleep there, away from my parents. For a few years, my older brother also came with me, but that stopped when he went to university. So from fourth grade to about ninth grade, I would sleep at the abandoned factory, and that was when I had real encounters with ghosts. I started to see ghost-like things and experience sleep paralysis in my elementary school days.

One time, when I woke up, I saw two black hands pushing down on my chest like this [*putting his arms on his chest*]. I was completely paralyzed while lying down and could not move my body. As I broke in a cold sweat, I desperately started thinking about how I could move my body. I remember thinking, "If I can twist my body and roll off the futon (Japanese mattress) onto the tatami mat (Japanese-style floor), maybe I can break free." So, I tried to move my body like this [*slightly leaning his body to the side*]. I struggled with all my might, but my voice would not come out either. I could not shout for help, so I got out of sleep paralysis by rolling over my body. This happened to me in my late elementary school years. So I was already having supernatural encounters.

I would then tell my friends at school about my spiritual experiences during recess, as children in my hometown did back in those days. In the town where I lived, which is located in the middle reaches of the Yoshino River in Tokushima, each class had about 40 to 50 students. I found that about five to six of them had also seen a ghost or a will-o'-the-wisp. None of my friends said, "Spirits aren't real. They are all made up." Elementary schoolers in the countryside couldn't logically explain that ghosts were unscientific or that ghost stories were unreliable. Many people who grew up in the city would argue like that, but elementary school students in the countryside would not. Rather, many of them shared their own experiences. I remember someone telling me, "I saw a will-o'-the-wisp flying above the mountain near my house."

The Yoshino River was near my house in Tokushima. Perhaps some of you visited the river and saw the submersible bridge from the Iwanohana Observatory on Shiroyama Mountain when you went on a pilgrimage to the Holy Land, Tokushima (One of the pilgrimage sites of Happy Science). When I was young, I often went fly-fishing for minnows in the evening by the downstream side of the submersible bridge on the Yoshino River. I remember one of my friends back then telling me that he saw a will-o'-the-wisp near that bridge. I have not seen one myself, but according to his story, it was so bright that when it drifted over the river, he could clearly see the riverbed. That tells us that a spirit gives off a certain intensity of light. He said that the will-o'-the-wisp was about one foot in size and had a certain brightness to it. This was at night. Others mentioned similar stories, too. When I was in elementary school, I spent a lot of time talking about ghosts with my friends in this way rather than studying. Back in those days, we did not have cram schools, so that is what we would do. It was around this time in the summer, like today.

Also, back in the day, I heard from some of my friends that they recently saw a bluish-white will-o'-the-wisp floating out from the roof of someone else's house. Then, one week later, their family member died. Its size and color varied depending on the person telling the story; some said they saw an orange light, while others said it was blue. In any case, people had this experience.

Since it was the countryside, even TV stations featured ghost stories during the summertime. In Kawashima Town, where I lived, the nearest train station is called Awa-Kawashima, and the station next to it is called Gaku. Gaku station is known for selling a set of five boarding tickets called "*Go-Nyu-Gaku* Tickets" as a lucky charm. (In Japanese, *Go* means "five" and in this context, "your." *Nyu-Gaku* means "to enroll." So, *Go-Nyu-Gaku* can mean "[I wish for] your [successful] enrollment.") There was a crematorium near the station and, one time, there was a rumor going around that a ghost had appeared there in the morning. Some media outlets, such as Shikoku Hoso Broadcasting and NHK (Japanese public broadcasting station), came to capture the ghost on camera and featured the topic on their morning shows. I, myself, was rather skeptical about the rumor. I found it strange that a ghost would appear at exactly 6:00 a.m. every morning. It turned out that somehow the sunrays lit up a corner of the crematorium, which people mistook for a ghost. So, I was right; it was not a ghost. In any case, I heard many ghost stories like that back then.

An episode with an elementary school teacher

One day, when I was telling my classmates about my spiritual experiences, the homeroom teacher from the next classroom came over and called me out. You may have already read this story in my book *Twiceborn* (New York: IRH Press, 2020). She asked me intimidatingly, "I heard you telling others about ghosts and saying things like humans have a soul. On what grounds are you saying such nonsense?" She knew that I was good at studying, so she confronted me and said that I should not be making unscientific claims. Apparently, she was very famous in Tokushima Prefecture for being active in the Japan Teachers' Union. A teacher like that stopped me and tried to talk me down.

I believe she was trying to convince me out of kindness. She probably wanted to tell me, "You are doing very well in your studies, so I don't want you to jeopardize your future by talking about the other world and ghosts, or by saying that humans are spiritual beings or that the other world exists. People who talk like that do worse in school or do not succeed after they graduate from school. So, I should nip your behavior in the bud." I think she tried to convince me out of goodwill in this way.

But I had witnessed two arms coming out of thin air and pressing down on my chest [*extending his arms out right in front of himself*] and then not being able to move, despite my desperate effort, as I broke out in a sweat. As someone who had experienced these things first-hand, I could never agree with her. Also, I was not the only one who saw spirits; other people had seen them, too. So, I told her, "But there are so many people who have seen spirits, so I simply think they exist." I never agreed with her, nor did I say that spirits don't exist.

That day, I went home and told my father, Honorary Advisor Saburo Yoshikawa, who passed away about seven years ago (at the time of the lecture), about what happened at school. Upon hearing it, he got angry and said, "Oh, she's a notorious activist of the Japan Teachers' Union. A schoolteacher mustn't teach such a lie!" He continued, "A schoolteacher must teach what is right. Why on earth are they teaching such a lie! This is unacceptable. They must always teach the right thing. If they teach mistaken ideas, children will grow up believing they are true."

My father had studied various religions when he was younger, and even had spiritual experiences himself, so he was convinced that spirits exist. He was the type of person who would deliberately go to the so-called "haunted spots" or "haunted houses" that were mentioned in magazines. Every time a haunted house was on the news, he would go and check it out himself saying, "With my willpower, the ghosts won't stand a chance." Even if I warned him not to go to spooky places like that, he would insist on going. Because he had undergone various spiritual experiences, he believed in the existence of the other world and spirits.

So, when I told my father that the Teachers' Union-affiliated teacher tried to persuade me by saying, "The other world does not exist. Spirits do not exist. Retract your opinions. Stop talking to your peers about them. Admit that you are wrong," but that I did not succumb to her, my father said, "Good. That's exactly what you should have done. A teacher must not teach mistaken ideas." I remember my father being very angry with the teacher. This is what I experienced in my elementary school days.

The mystery of a family that underwent a series of misfortunes

On the contrary, I had the opposite experience during my freshman year in high school. As I previously said, in elementary school, there was a teacher who did not believe in spiritual matters, but during my freshman year of high school, I met a teacher who believed in them. If I remember correctly, he taught classical Japanese, and according to what I later heard, he was a believer of a Japanese religious group called *Seicho-no-Ie*. He would insert strange, spiritual stories into his classical Japanese class and skillfully propagate the teachings of his religion. We, students, could not tell, but apparently, he did this during class.

Here is one of the episodes he told us about. A family had been going through a series of misfortunes, including its members becoming ill. They found the events odd and suspected an evil spiritual influence, so they called someone with spiritual abilities to investigate the matter. The person brought a pot full of hot water and walked around the house. He entered every room on the first and second floors, and the water started simmering when he moved across certain places. The water boiled in certain areas but stopped in others. The boiling indicated that "something" was there. A malicious spirit or evil spirit made the water boil all of a sudden.

The teacher told us this story in class, and I remember thinking, "What a strange teacher." Classical Japanese literature has many stories that involve curses, vengeful spirits, and *ikiryo* (a spirit of a living person), so perhaps it was not so strange for him to be familiar with these subjects. In any case, this teacher would insert spiritual stories during class to propagate his religion. Apparently, he was the district leader of Seicho-no-Ie in Tokushima Prefecture. I remember thinking that teachers can be so different depending on what they believe.

The content of my books proves they are not fabricated

It has already been 29 years since I first had a spiritual experience—not the ones I had in my elementary school days, but the automatic writing that started in my twenties—and started to receive spiritual revelations and messages from the Spirit World. And it has been 24 years since I decided to walk this path and launch a religious movement. I have so far published 600 books (at the time of the lecture; as of December 2025, over 3,250 books had been published) including the translated versions that are published worldwide.

If you look at the content of my books, you will see that they cannot be fabrications. If you read a certain amount, let's say 10 to 20 books, you will understand that these messages came down from the other world, indeed. So you cannot say that there is a 50-50 chance of spirits and the other world being real; they are either 100 percent true or 100 percent false. As someone who has repeatedly undergone spiritual experiences, I definitely cannot deny the existence of the Spirit World.

2

Why Was Spirituality Excluded from Academic Studies?

René Descartes and Immanuel Kant separated the spirit from the body

In this lifetime, I was chosen to stand in a position to teach the spiritual truth, which was unexpected at the beginning. Fortunately, I was the type of person who believed in spiritual matters, but of course, as a child, I was not fully convinced about them yet.

Even though I believed in spiritual existences, I also did relatively well in school and achieved a lot. Since I did well in all subjects and people recognized me for that, I was able to show people that I was not crazy in an earthly sense. Even after acquiring spiritual abilities, I worked as a productive member of society at the trading house where I was employed. I even worked in New York City and spoke English. Therefore, the first half of my life proved in various ways that I was not deluded in a worldly sense. I personally believe that I was guided spiritually to lead such a life. In other words, I believe I was put through intense intellectual training to make sure that I would be capable in a worldly sense, as well.

A similar episode is mentioned in this book (*Spirituality and Education*) regarding Emanuel Swedenborg. He awakened to the existence of the spiritual world in his 50s, and by that time, he had already made tremendous accomplishments in this world. He was a well-known scientist and a key figure of his time. A person like him suddenly awakened to the Spirit World and began exploring it. What he achieved after his awakening were, in fact, far greater than what he had done before then.

On the other hand, Immanuel Kant did not have any spiritual experiences during his lifetime (according to his spiritual message). So, he could only deepen his thoughts about God, the other world, and other metaphysical matters intellectually. It seems that Jean-Jacques Rousseau did not have any spiritual experiences, either.

If you go further back in time, before Kant, there was René Descartes, the father of modern Western philosophy. He taught the theory of "mind-body dualism," which became the source of Western thought that considers the spiritual body and the physical body separately. For example, in hospitals and clinics, doctors ignore the soul because they are just treating the physical body. This attitude began with Descartes. Descartes himself possessed spiritual abilities. He often received revelations through dreams and traveled to the Spirit World in his sleep. He was the type of person who could receive spiritual revelations. However, he presented the idea of separating the spirit from the body in his book, *Discourse on the Method*. Kant shared the same approach. He excluded things that could not be experienced by everyone from academic studies, and instead, only explored things that could be confirmed by everyone through means like scientific experiments. This thought began to spread, and was known later as the philosophy of Enlightenment.

As the movement became popular, it liberated people from the constraints of traditional religions, but at the same time, it produced a negative outcome. Even though the original intention was simply to remove spiritual matters from the subject of academic research, people of later generations developed a tendency to deny anything that could not be experienced.

The reason many Buddhist monks and scholars are atheists and materialists

This kind of thinking has persisted for a long time, and along the way, various ways of thinking that incorporated Kant's ideas branched off to form Neo-Kantianism. The scholars at the Department of Religious Studies and the Department of Buddhist Studies at the University of Tokyo have been strongly influenced by this idea. In their research on Buddhism, they are doing their best to interpret Buddhist ideas in a materialistic way. Even though Buddhist scriptures often mention spirits and the other world, these scholars cut out those parts as much as possible and only keep the parts that make sense in this world. This is because they are afraid of becoming a laughingstock by interpreting those descriptions literally. They disregard the spiritual aspect to make themselves look as scholarly as possible. They have narrowed down the scope of research in this way. That is why people who studied at those universities and became monks in Buddhist temples are mostly atheists and materialists. This is the case even more for those who studied at Buddhist universities.

There is a school of Buddhism called Zen Buddhism, which simply teaches people to sit quietly, but Shakyamuni Buddha was not just sitting for the sake of sitting. You often see religious practitioners sitting on rocks by the Ganges River, but there is nothing admirable about just sitting there. It would actually be more productive to go fishing than to just sit there. If they are going to sit on the rocks, they might as well be fishing; then they could at least provide a side dish for dinner for themselves sometimes. People sit and meditate, but what would make their practice truly great is if they entered a meditative state and sensed something spiritual. Those who cannot understand this and merely sit there and meditate are doing nothing more than just sitting.

Zen Buddhism has largely been reduced to just protocols and methods. A great number of their practitioners do not have any real spiritual experiences, and even if they do, they tend to flatly deny them as delusions. When they practice the "Meditation to Think of Nothing," all they do is aim to empty their minds. However, if the ultimate goal of this mediation was simply to think about nothing, Buddhism would never have spread to become a world religion. Considering that Shakyamuni Buddha gave so many teachings, you can assume that the meditation he did allowed countless amounts of inspiration and revelations to flow to him from the heavenly world.

Recently, in Japan, there was a Diet member who demanded the declassification of information about UFOs. Apparently, the document he submitted included a description from a Buddhist scripture that said Shakyamuni Buddha met and spoke with the *Myojo Tenshi* (deity of the morning star). Since Myojo refers to Venus, he claimed that Shakyamuni Buddha spoke with a space person from Venus. Based on this, one of the Diet members demanded that the government disclose information about UFOs. Leaving aside its authenticity, it is indeed true that Shakyamuni Buddha had many such spiritual experiences.

3
Academic Studies Must Be Built Upon the Idea that Materialism Is Wrong

Buddha's dialogues with devils and gods are true stories

If you interpret the Buddhist scriptures literally, you will see many gods, Sakra, and devils appearing and having conversations with Shakyamuni Buddha. Buddha's dialogues with devils and gods (compiled in *The Samyutta Nikaya*) are handed down to this day, and you can easily find them in bookstores in Japan. Even so, Buddhist scholars do not consider them to be the truth but as mere psychological descriptions or folk tales.

But they are true stories. It is better to simply take them as something that actually happened because that is the closest to the Truth. Why would these dialogues need to be fabricated? There is no reason for that. The fact that they have remained for 2,500 years means that Shakyamuni Buddha spoke with devils and gods. This is the simplest way that makes sense. Why would someone have to invent such stories and write them down in play-like dialogues? It is better to accept them as written.

People who have had no spiritual experiences tend to deny them, but for those who have, they are natural events. The scriptures simply describe how Buddha responded to what the devils or gods said.

This is exactly what I am doing when I receive spiritual messages. It is indeed possible to have a conversation with spirits. I have been experiencing these spiritual phenomena first-hand for a long time and still am to this day.

If academic studies are meant to pursue what the Truth is, we must place what is right at the foundation of academics. The Truth is that it is wrong to deny the existence of the other world and spirits and think that physical matters are all there is in this world. Therefore, academic studies must also be built upon this Truth. It is the mundane nature of mediocre human beings that eliminates this foundation from academics.

Socrates told many stories about reincarnation and the other world

In fact, this is not only an issue in religion but also in philosophy. Without question, the father of Greek philosophy is Socrates, but he himself did not write any books. It was his disciple, Plato, who wrote many books about him. Plato was 40 years younger than him. According to Plato, Socrates' words were full of stories about the reincarnation of the soul and the other world.

It is recorded that Socrates had a guardian spirit called "Daemon." The guardian spirit did not always tell him what to do, but would stop him when he was about to do something wrong. Socrates lived faithfully to the words of his guardian spirit. Toward the end of his life, he was tried in the People's Court and was sentenced to death on the charge of corrupting people. This was not necessarily an attack from the atheists. In fact, he was accused of spreading baseless ideas that came from his experience with his inner god, rather than believing in the traditional gods of Greece. In modern language, it would be called "the sin of starting a new cult." He was put on trial for spreading the words of the god he conversed with, instead of revering the ancient, traditional gods. Back then, introducing new gods was considered an ideological crime that deserved the death sentence. When Socrates was jailed, even the prison guards told him to flee, and his disciples prepared for him to escape by boat. However, his guardian spirit, Daemon, stayed quiet throughout and did not say a word this one time. It did not tell him to flee or stop him from doing anything; nor did it respond to any of Socrates' questions about what to do. Socrates understood from this that he was meant to die. So, he accepted his destiny and drank the poison hemlock.

The fact that this story has been handed down for over 2,000 years is proof that he did not compromise but lived true to the Truth. He never gave in. He stuck to the Truth as the Truth and to what is right as what is right. Although he was over 70 years old, he had two children who were still very young. Everyone was pleading with Socrates to escape and they even bribed the prison guards, but he declined them all and chose to die. I believe Socrates was mindful of how this event would be seen and judged in the future, so he stayed faithful to the decision of his guardian spirit.

This was the original nature of philosophy, but modern scholars have disregarded all of these spiritual experiences. What's more, philosophy from the 1900s has become much like symbolic logic or a "philosophy of mathematicians." This shows how a lack of spiritual experience can lead academic studies astray.

4
The Ideal Education Lies in Developing the Soul

The true nature of human beings is the soul

In a sense, academic studies have now become very rational and practical. However, the point is whether they are based on the Truth. People may believe that they are building academic scholarship based on a sturdy, concrete-like foundation, but in truth, what they believe as a concrete foundation is a mirage and what they believe as fraudulent is the Truth. This is what I have been teaching all these years.

We have also just embarked on a "fight for the Truth" in the field of education. If people receive religious education in their childhood or in relatively early stages where they can learn from their teachers open-heartedly, they will be able to accept spiritual matters without much resistance, even as they grow into adulthood. However, if they grow up hearing that the other world does not exist and that those who believe in spiritual matters are superstitious or absurd—which are the common narratives of journalism—they will criticize people who are attracted to spirituality or religion. These people tend to say things like, "You are weird," or "You are being scammed."

However, everyone will eventually have to reap what they sow. Ultimately, people will have to face necessary consequences when they die and return to the other world; they will see for themselves what the Truth is. Of course, the recent spiritual messages reveal that, when people die, those who did not believe in the other world while they were alive have no idea that they have died, even after becoming spirits. This includes people who had higher social standings, such as the prime ministers or presidents of a country. Those who did not know or believe in spiritual matters while they were alive do not accept the existence of the afterlife even after they have died. They keep insisting, "I'm still conscious, so I must be alive." They continue to think, "I'm just confined in some place or lost somewhere. Perhaps I'm hallucinating. I'm not sure what's going on, but either way, I'm still alive." They cannot even explain to themselves what is happening.

There is the so-called "left-wing education." Literature with left-wing ideologies does not mention spiritual matters or the other world, so you won't have a chance to learn anything about the afterlife. No matter how much you study literature or philology of such kind, you won't find any explanations about the afterlife, so none of the knowledge you acquire by studying it will help you in the other world. The only thing you can take back with you to the other world is your mind, or your soul. Indeed, everything must start with the truth that *the true nature of human beings is the soul.* Therefore, an ideal education is one that develops the human soul. It is essential to build a society where people strive to develop themselves in a spiritual sense and contribute to creating a prosperous world.

We recently founded the Happy Science Academy in Nasu (in Tochigi Prefecture), and the first semester just finished (at the time of the lecture). I sense a new beginning coming. At this school, students who are good at studies in a worldly sense also have deep religious faith and receive a religious education. According to recent research by an educational publisher, both junior high and high school students of the Happy Science Academy have received a standard deviation score of 65, which is the equivalent of the prestigious schools in Tokyo. These excellent students are also receiving a proper religious education.

We are planning to establish Happy Science Academy in Kansai as well, and its location has almost been decided. As it will soon be announced officially, it is scheduled to open in 2013. (Happy Science Academy Kansai opened in April 2013.) After that, we also have plans to establish Happy Science University in 2016*. We are determined to carry out and fulfill the sacred mission to provide religious education and produce faithful people who are capable at work and can contribute to society. Religion must not be considered a superstition. It must have a real presence in society and be helpful to people. This is the change I want to bring about.

Happy Science educates working adults

If we were to conduct a survey or take a poll on whether people believe in the other world, the majority of people would probably say they do not. But I think most people are not sure deep down. So, I would like these people to just trust me and believe my words.

I have written over 600 books (at the time of the lecture)
To prove that the other world exists.
I am continuing to write more books now.
They are not Buddhist scriptures from ancient times
Or philosophies from old times.
They are being written now—in the present.
I have published spiritual messages from various spirits.
About 100 have already been published
This year alone (2010).
The spirits all have different personalities.
They have different characters
And different ways of thinking.
I am releasing their messages

To prove the existence of the other world.
I am trying to prove something that is hard to prove.

So, please believe that the other world exists,
That the true nature of human beings is the soul,
That this world is a training ground,
That after death,
You will return to an appropriate place in the other world
Based on the spiritual training you underwent
In this earthly world,
And that the way you live in this life will determine
Where you go in the afterlife.
Put simply, this is all I am saying.

Happy Science is a place that teaches you how to live your life in this world based on the truth that souls exist. In this sense, Happy Science educates working adults. We teach children, too, but people over 100 years old are also studying here. You do not learn the knowledge we teach in school. So, unless you acquire this knowledge as an adult, you will never come to know it. If you are going to learn it you will need to be taught it by someone or through something.

You may have friends or acquaintances who kindly give you Happy Science books or take you to a Happy Science movie. Please try not to miss out on these opportunities.

These people are truly doing so from the goodness of their hearts. I have seen countless people become lost after death and are clueless about why they are suffering. So, I want to teach people more than ever that *knowledge is power*.

[Editor's note]
Happy Science University (HSU) opened in 2015. It is an advanced educational institution that originated in Japan.

CHAPTER THREE

Why Is It a Problem to Live a Self-Centered Life?

—The Essential Mindset to Get Out of Unhappiness

Recorded in Japanese on August 13, 2019
at Happy Science Special Lecture Hall.
English translation.

1

Why Do People Become Self-Centered?

A self-centered life is a life of self-protection

Today, I would like to talk about the theme, "Why is it a problem to live a self-centered life?" I have decided to talk about this because I still find this problem in many people and places even after conducting Happy Science activities for more than 30 years. Many people lead self-centered lives because they believe it is more beneficial to live that way. Many people probably think instinctively that they were born to gain some kind of benefit in life. Oftentimes, they are not aware that they are self-centered even though others around them feel they are. When others see them as being self-centered they just believe they are being smart. Because they see themselves as smart, they believe they can figure out the shortest and quickest way to catch their "prey," to score higher points, or to gain a better reputation, and they believe this is the right thing to do.

I have put it in the modern context, but to use an old expression, a self-centered life is a life of self-protection. All living creatures, including humans, animals, and insects, possess an instinct to protect themselves from their enemies.

When we face the danger of annihilation, we think about running away from them if we are weak, and we think about defeating them if we are strong. Most people act this way. From the time we are born as babies, we preoccupy ourselves with how to avoid getting hurt, abused, or abandoned as we live in a world run by adults. This is a necessary instinct for us to survive in this world.

A self-centered attitude can be observed in some races and nations as well

A self-centered attitude can be observed not only in individuals but in whole races and nations as well. I will not give specific names because that is not the main point of this lecture, but there are a few near Japan. These countries constantly denounce and criticize others while glorifying themselves. I wonder how they can be so confident in what they say, but in any case, they utterly criticize and denounce the actions and remarks of other countries. At the same time, they glorify their own, boast about themselves, and treat their leaders as gods. If we take a look at the countries around Japan alone, there are a few like this. The nerve they have is beyond me. They express their attitude in their newspapers and public broadcasting.

In Japan, this attitude is not common. The same is true in the West. Of course, their media may sometimes say or write things to make their countries look better or to commend their countries, but they are usually critical of their government and leaders in power. Many mass media outlets are critical of the strong and protective of the weak. But in totalitarian-oriented countries, mass media outlets that criticize the strong and protect the weak are regarded as dangerous to the government. The government cannot allow media like that to co-exist, so they put pressure on them to prevent them from writing or saying anything critical.

I will not get into too much detail because this is not the main topic of today's lecture, but I am sure some countries would feel ashamed of their attitude if they honestly reflected on their behavior. At a glance, it may appear smart and more beneficial to commend their own country and denigrate other countries. It may sound exciting and can make their citizens fanatical or feel intoxicated. These tendencies can show up even in democratic countries that are founded on fascism or Nazism. In general, these countries boast about how they are wonderful people of excellent bloodline or are a superior race, and talk down to other countries. Sometimes, they even persecute other races.

After hearing me talk about it in this much detail, you can probably understand what I am trying to say. I am not sure if it is appropriate to compare a personal issue with a national issue that could even cause wars, but I am using this analogy to make it easier for you to understand. For example, the Nazis discriminated against Jewish people by labeling them as bad and persecuting them. By trying to completely eradicate their enemy, the Nazis tried to elevate the pride and superiority of the Aryan race, thereby bringing unity to the country and making it stronger.

The difficulty of building a good relationship with self-centered people

A similar tendency can also be observed in individuals. Some people quickly boast about how great, wonderful, and accomplished they are, yet belittle others, drag them down, and criticize them. It is often very difficult to get along with people like this. These types of people, who praise themselves but criticize others, are most likely sensitive and vulnerable to criticism. So if you are too kind to them, they will often misinterpret your kindness. They have this kind of complicated side to them. If you are very religious and you happen to treat them too kindly or praise them out of sympathy, they will suddenly change their attitude and become arrogant or conceited. So, they are indeed very difficult to deal with.

Usually, when people are praised, they tend to be humble and say that they were just lucky or that others have helped them. This is how an ordinary person behaves. But there are people who say, "I know. There are many reasons why I'm so great," and start boasting on and on. Although there isn't such a high percentage of people like this, at least one in 10 people has this tendency.

If their boasting gets out of hand, the people around them will start to dislike them. When they notice this and feel hurt for being disliked, some of them will think twice about bragging, whereas others will end up becoming depressed and hole themselves up or try to escape from reality. These people, who were once aggressive toward others, will suddenly start belittling themselves. They switch from being a sadist to being a masochist and beat themselves up, scolding themselves by saying, "I'm no good."

There is still hope if their low self-esteem makes them reflect on themselves. They can correct their mistakes by reflecting on their past behavior. However, if they are the type of person who does not like to self-reflect and instead prefers to take it out on others, they are likely to attack people again when they next see them, in an effort to make up for their low self-esteem. They will criticize or speak ill of them with even more severity than they did before in an effort to satisfy their hunger for recognition. As they repeat this kind of behavior, they end up developing a kind of social phobia, having trust issues, or becoming untrustworthy. This makes it very difficult for them to cultivate good relationships with other people.

Having seen and heard about these types of people, I have offered many teachings on interpersonal relationships, but they seem to have a hard time understanding them.

2
The Difference in People's Mindset

People who lived for the sake of others, the world, and the future of humanity

• Jesus Christ and Socrates

If we take self-centeredness as self-protection, it is something that animals, plants, insects, and humans all naturally have as a common instinct. This means that it is rare to find people in this world who have surpassed this instinct.

These kinds of people sometimes exist, but they are beyond the understanding of those who lead earthly lives. People who lead unworldly lives seem to put themselves at a disadvantage, but they do this for the sake of others, the world, and the future of humanity. Their behaviors are incomprehensible to people who live secular lives.

Take Jesus Christ, for example. Secular people probably think, "I don't understand how someone could save humanity by being crucified. He should have thought more about himself. He should have fled."

Socrates is another figure whom people can hardly understand. After he was given a death sentence for corrupting the youth and falsifying God, he killed himself by drinking poison hemlock even though he had the opportunity to escape from prison. If he had escaped, it would have implied that he was a liar, so he chose to die for the Truth instead. He thought there was no need for someone who said the right thing to run away. He believed that a truthful life would remain in history forever. However, people who fail to understand his aspirations probably see his life as one of absurdity.

Nowadays, people rush into the department store like wild animals to find the best deals when a sale is on. They go to big sales thinking that they need to be one step ahead of everyone else to get the best deals. They instinctively feel joy and happiness if they win against fellow competitors. But there are also people, although rare, who do not live that way. Many of their names have not remained so only some of them are still known to this day.

• Shakyamuni Buddha

Shakyamuni Buddha is another example. No Buddhists ever talk badly about Shakyamuni Buddha, but if we travel back in time and observe him objectively, we will see that he abandoned his parents, wife, and child and had his hair cut off to become a monk, despite being born as a prince of a small kingdom. He then spent six years in the forest undergoing ascetic training, including fasting, in pursuit of the Truth. He eventually became just skin and bones with his veins protruding before he attained enlightenment. He aspired to spiritually awaken many people, not only the people in his time but also those of later generations, through his enlightenment.

If I was a weekly magazine reporter in his time, I could have written many gossip articles about him. Like the modern mass media, I could have written, for example, "Prince of Shakya Kingdom abandons his throne and goes missing!" When Siddhartha left the palace on his horse named Kanthaka to become a monk, he switched clothes with Chandaka, his loyal servant and charioteer. It was his way of telling everyone that he had renounced his secular life. He then became a monk by having his hair cut off near the river.

If you were to describe this in the way a weekly tabloid would, you would call Siddhartha an idiot. Based on common sense, you could say, "What will become of his aging father?" "What a pity for his stepmother who took care of him," or "His wife deserves the most pity. She must be at a loss for words considering her husband left her soon after she gave birth to their child. A social outcast like him should not be able to attain enlightenment and be called Buddha!" Weekly tabloids like *Bunshun* and *Shincho* would accuse him of things like this in whatever way they like. This is how people may have seen him back then. In the worldly sense, Siddhartha's actions would be considered losses and he would be criticized by society, so no ordinary person would do those things.

Later, Shakyamuni Buddha accepted about 500 youths from the Shakya Kingdom to join his order as monks, which eventually led to the fall of the Shakya Kingdom. Because many sons of powerful noble families became monks, the Shakya Kingdom declined and was ultimately conquered by the Kosala Kingdom. Then it was destroyed in the not-too-distant future.

People have different views of this outcome. Some say that the Shakya Kingdom may have survived if Siddhartha had become its king. Others suspect that the Shakya Kingdom would have been destroyed regardless because it was surrounded by two powerful kingdoms, the Kosala Kingdom and the Magadha Kingdom. Then, others say that Siddhartha accepted the 500 young men precisely because he foresaw that his kingdom was destined to fall. People say various things because the way Siddhartha behaved was beyond their comprehension. I am sure that he transcended all of the criticisms he faced in this world and was looking a long way into the future. He was aiming for something infinitely far in the distance that was beyond people's imagination.

A prince who murdered his father to achieve his ambitions quickly

From a worldly perspective, it is common sense to choose a path that is most beneficial to oneself. Siddhartha, too, could have pressured his aging father into abdicating quickly to give way to him, instead of leaving the palace to become a monk. That way, he could have gained power and freedom while he was still young. If he felt, "I'm tired of this life. I can't stand being constantly watched as the prince and having to obey my parents. I don't like being surrounded by many wives, who were wedded to me so that I can't leave the castle. I'm sick of the evening banquets. People are trying to immerse me in pleasure by constantly holding banquets. I've had enough," he could have driven the king into retiring and succeeded the throne instead of leaving the castle and becoming a monk.

In fact, this is what Prince Ajatashatru of the powerful Magadha Kingdom did. He killed his own father to achieve his ambitions. He confined his father in jail and forbade his men from feeding him. But after a while, his father did not die, which he found strange, so he kept watch. He found that his mother would lather herself with food, such as flour and butter, every time she went to see her husband and kept him nourished that way. So, Prince Ajatashatru put his mother in jail as well and attempted to kill her. However, the minister stopped him and told him. "In the long history of India, although there have been instances of princes killing the king, there has never been a case of a prince killing his own mother. You should not leave a stain on your name like this." Therefore, he decided to give his mother food while she was kept in confinement. Her name was Kosala Devi. She believed in Shakyamuni Buddha, so she prayed to him, and this became the origin of the Three Pure Land Sutras. Various dramas unfolded around these events.

People like Ajatashatru probably believe that smart people can find the shortest and quickest ways to achieve their ambitions. When they manage to swiftly achieve their ambitions in the most efficient way, they become proud of themselves and believe they deserve other people's praise. This is what they usually think. Of course, people can sometimes achieve their goals using these approaches. For example, an executive could frame the CEO and drag them down out of a desire to become the CEO themselves as soon as possible. Or an actress aiming to be the top star could intentionally spread a scandalous rumor about the current top star in order to dethrone her. People sometimes resort to various means to achieve their ambitions.

Heavenly spirits with excessive jealousy will fall to lower dimensions

Now, let us shift our attention to the world of hell. In hell, no one praises other people. All they do is speak ill of, swear at, or curse people. They say things like, "I'll kill you" or "I'll make you lose your mind." The spirits in hell who do compliment other people are, in most cases, swindlers. You can find people like them in this earthly world, too. They compliment people with an ulterior motive, for instance, to get something from them or to ruin them. The people who did this while they were alive are now in hell. If the spirits in hell happen to come across such spirits, they may be tricked and sent to an even deeper hell to undergo a tougher level of spiritual discipline. You need to know that, in hell, only frauds compliment people. In general, spirits in hell only speak ill of people or verbally abuse them.

In heaven, those who constantly and candidly speak ill of others will not be able to remain in the world. Of course, even outstanding people can occasionally develop a degree of jealousy in their minds. They may criticize others or talk badly about them out of jealousy, but it is not so much of a problem if their criticisms are kept to an acceptable level. Each person has their own quirks and retains their personality even after returning to heaven, so they may not like a particular person because of their quirks.

The rivals you did not like may have returned to heaven if they were of excellent character. Two rival singers, for example, may reside in the same dimension of heaven. Each of them will be different because of their individual characters, so one of the singers might criticize the other by saying, "Her singing is no good. She doesn't sing this part or that part well." Criticisms like this can be justified to a certain extent if they contain lessons that help the other singer improve. If that is the case, the person criticizing can stay where they are in heaven.

However, if they develop jealousy that is too intense for them to control, the ground below them—being the ground of the fourth, fifth, sixth, seventh, or eighth dimension—will suddenly crack open and they will fall straight into a lower world. So, while you may think it is impossible for a crack to form in the ground, if you become overly jealous of someone, the ground you stand on will split open and you will no longer be able to stay in the dimension you are in. You will fall through the crack to a lower dimension. If you grow extremely jealous, you might even fall all the way down to hell.

It is possible for spirits in heaven to suddenly disappear. This could either mean that they have fallen to a lower dimension or that they have ascended to a higher dimension. If spirits in heaven put on a heroic act or behave in a way that is praiseworthy, they will be told, "You have completed your current level of spiritual training," and be taken up to a higher dimension. But there are also cases where spirits fall to lower dimensions. So, please be mindful to control your jealousy.

3
The Common Pitfall of Self-Centered People

The problems that smart but self-centered people face related to aptitude

• They tend to spot other people's shortcomings

I have mentioned that self-centered people can be smart in an earthly sense and tend to gain benefits and results relatively quickly. But they can also be quick to spot other people's shortcomings. This is a common pitfall. They all face it; there are hardly any exceptions. As you study a lot, you will be able to quickly find what other people are struggling with. You can easily see the areas that others are weak in or what they are having trouble with. So, as you excel in your studies, you tend to spot other people's mistakes rather quickly. This tendency starts to show during middle school and high school and continues into university. Some people even display this tendency in the workplace. This is one of the pitfalls that smart people face. Please be aware that you need to overcome this tendency.

During middle school or high school, you will indeed feel good if you get good grades, are the head of the student council, or are respected as the class valedictorian. But, with this level of aptitude, you will also be able to see the shortcomings in others. If you are a bright student, your peers and teachers will tend to praise and respect you regardless of your character, so you will not realize that you have this distorted part within you. Once you enter university, however, you may be criticized by some for your bad character, and when you start job hunting, your character will be assessed more. In Japan, usually, the job interview is done by the university alumni working in the company, and they have observed many new graduates over the years. They check to see whether the candidate has a good character, is highly motivated, and is not foulmouthed. They will not hire a new graduate who they think is still immature. A person's character also has a great influence on whether the new employee is eligible for promotion.

So, it is not just being smart that matters. A person can be smart, but if they have a negative character, they should never become a leader. If someone like that is at the top, everyone working under them will be discouraged. Let me give you an example. There are some leaders who constantly speak ill of others over drinks. If they pressure their subordinates into agreeing with them and the subordinates say equally bad things to maintain harmony in their workplace, this will definitely lead to problems. These people must not hold the position of a superior.

To do well in society, people must not only have an acceptable level of work ability but must also have good character. Students who were well-respected for getting good grades need to check to see if they have built good character; otherwise, they may have a hard time getting a promotion or building good relationships with others.

• They tend to blame others or their own environment

When things do not go as they wish, people with aptitude tend to misuse their smartness to blame others or their environment. They may blame other people by saying, "I'm in this situation because of him. It's his fault. He is tattling on me to my superior. He is trying to prevent me from becoming successful."

Or perhaps they may blame the environment and say, for example, "Our business is not going well because GDP is not increasing. So, it's not my fault that we're doing poorly." However, in any given economic situation, there will be a mix of companies that are constantly growing and those that are going out of business. Some companies close even in a good economy whereas others continue to grow during a recession. In any of these circumstances, some people will work hard while others do not want to bear responsibility and will just blame other people or their environment.

Mafia-like cunningness

The problem with the above types of people is that they cannot take other people's advice. They are sometimes told things like, "You need to improve this point," "Your department or section is not doing well, so I advise you to do it this way," "Why don't you come to work earlier?" or "Read proper books. Make more effort to read at least the politics and society section of the newspaper." But when they are told, for example, "Our negotiation with that company failed the other day because your tongue slipped," they will only retort, "Don't blame me for your failure." People with bad character say things like that shamelessly and leave others dumbfounded. They will not listen to what other people tell them and instead just respond with, "You're a bad person for bad-mouthing me." So, the people around them will gradually stop giving them advice and stay away from them. Then, because they have been left alone, they will think, "Everyone is so cold. They are abusing me. This world is like hell. I am the only one working so hard with good intentions, but everyone is putting up a cold front and bullying me. I can't stand this."

When you give advice to a self-centered person to help them improve their personality or behavior, they always shoot back at you and say that you are mean, ill-willed, or wrong. You could say that these people are quick thinkers. Although some of them are smart in the right sense of the word, others are smart in the opposite sense. Their idea of "clever" is similar to the cunningness of someone in the mafia or a gang member. These sly people are very good at starting quarrels. They twist your own words against you. In fact, this is what the mass media often do as well; they use your own remarks to lure you into their trap.

Mafia-like cunningness means being able to pick up some of what you say and use it against you. In this sense, they are smart. They have the wit to retort quickly. Let's say you got into an accident on the road. You were following the law, but the other driver broke the law and crashed into you. If you point this out to them, they will be defiant and say, "It's you who is wrong. It's your fault for coming here in the first place. Why on earth did you come here?" They will come up with all kinds of reasons to put the blame on you. If you happen to get into a quarrel with them late at night, they will say, "It's your fault for being here so late at night." Regardless, if you encounter them late in the afternoon, they will tell you, "It's your fault for walking around here so early in the evening to go drinking. You got into an accident because you were careless." Then, they will go on and say things like, "Give me your wallet. If you don't want to die, hand it over." If they find out that you have ¥300,000 (about $2,000) in it, they will tell you, "It's your fault for carrying so much money with you. If you didn't want someone to take it, you shouldn't have had it on you in the first place. I'm going to keep it for you," and then they will take your money anyway.

They take advantage of anything they can to benefit themselves. There are many spirits like them in hell. It is full of spirits like this. Devils and demons always stir up trouble by taking advantage of what you say and making you believe that you are the one to be blamed. So, you could say that they are quick-witted. It is best to stay away from them. Do not go to places where people like them gather and, instead, live among sound people.

If you happen to come across mafia-like people, prepare yourself for the worst and find a way out with minimal interaction. This is an important attitude to have because if you choose to confront them head-on, you could be in for a real bloodshed. They have deceived a lot of people, so they understand many different types of people. That is why honest or white-collar-type people will get themselves into deep trouble if they get caught up with mafia-like troublemakers. Even in hell, you could be involved in a real tragedy if you happen to encounter them.

Leaders must overcome their desire for self-protection and experience an awakening

I have observed many kinds of people, including those who have gone to hell and those who are likely to go there after death. As I said in the beginning, what they all have in common is the desire to protect themselves. If I were to tell them they are self-centered, they would snap back at me and refuse to accept it. On hearing this, they may turn defiant and say, "What is wrong with protecting myself?"

Of course, there is no problem with having a desire to protect yourself. In the process of becoming adults, children will learn how to protect themselves. Parents and teachers teach children how to protect themselves and survive in this world without getting injured, getting into an accident, or making mistakes at work, and live independently in society. As children grow older, they will take this further and learn how to protect their future families as well, such as their wife and children. This is the basic thinking they should have to live as humans.

In addition to this, some people will stand in the position of bearing greater responsibilities as leaders. When you stand above others, you must have superior abilities, the strength to protect others, and a heart of giving love. These qualities are extremely important.

This is true in any field you work in. Take doctors, for example. Each of them had to beat others in a tough competition to get into medical school and then pass the national exam to earn their license to practice medicine, but then they all eventually gain different reputations as doctors. They compete with each other in their hospital and can struggle with interpersonal relationships. Doctors who maintain harmonious relationships are evaluated highly, while those who do not are not.

There is a doctor-turned-critic named Hideki Wada. He graduated from Nada High School and entered Natural Sciences III at the University of Tokyo. After graduating, he continued to study at the university as a resident physician. It seems that he felt that the professor there was jealous of him. In one of his books, he wrote about how a "crazy" professor once put him in a nelson hold, dragged him into the office, and tried to choke him. After experiencing this, he quit working at the university hospital and started working at a private clinic. At the same time, he started writing books as a psychiatrist, appearing on TV, and doing other activities as a critic.

The "crazy" professor probably saw Dr. Wada as a cheeky student who did not listen to him. It is a little hard to believe that an older doctor who graduated from the University of Tokyo as well tried to choke a younger doctor, but I remember reading such an episode. I understand how the senior doctor must have felt. Dr. Wada wrote many books and voiced a lot of opinions, so he was probably rude. Perhaps he should have been more respectful to his seniors. But the incident may have motivated him to go independent. I believe there are many similar cases like this.

So, you need to experience an awakening. You can train yourself to develop greater abilities than others, obtain a more favorable position that allows you to achieve your ambitions, and strive to get a good job. With a good academic record, you probably managed to find work in various fields or work as a specialist or researcher. But after that, you need to go one step further and study life, people, and society more deeply.

4
Changing the Unhappy Mindset

Using underhanded means is not intelligence but a sin

At Happy Science, we teach people to love, nurture, and forgive others, but it is not easy to do. When people think of love, they often think of "love that takes." Many people think of love as winning over someone they like and, therefore, that love is something they take from others. They believe that smart people can take love from others very quickly. Some people even believe that winning over a person who is already in a relationship brings even greater happiness. They find double the pleasure in doing whatever they can to "steal" someone who is admired by others or who is already committed to someone else. But Happy Science teaches the complete opposite.

This is a difficult issue. You could say that the desire to steal love is part of the legacy of a competitive society. Wanting what others want or "hunting" and chasing after someone who runs away from you is love that loots, takes, confiscates, and steals. Countless people believe that the ability to do this shows how smart they are; they enjoy the dynamics of doing so or find it exciting to have their inner hunter brought out. They believe that love is something they get, like getting money in their pocket or having treasure in their hands.

To use an animal as an example, this is similar to snatching an egg from a hen and eating it, like a fox digging a hole to get into a chicken coop and steal a freshly laid egg from a chicken before the barn owner can collect it in the morning. For the fox, it would be exciting beyond words because it would mean that it outsmarted the human. The owner wonders, "Huh? Maybe the chicken didn't lay an egg today," while the fox gloats to himself, "I snatched the egg before he did. I'm smarter than him. Hehe." This is an analogy that describes the behavior of people who steal others' love. The fox may be overjoyed for successfully snatching an egg, but taking it without the right to do so will create problems because the owner worked hard to feed the chicken and care for it so that it would be able to lay an egg.

People who use their intelligence to cheat or who use underhanded methods to get what they want, or people who proactively try to learn this kind of knowledge from those around them will, sadly, just end up being as wily as the famous fictional thief, Lupin the Third. Their actions will be regarded as crimes and they will be chased forever by Inspector Zenigata. If they want an egg that is not theirs, they need to pay for it. That is commonly accepted behavior. Despite that, many people have a tendency to behave like a fox.

My episode with a fortune-teller

I had always been the type to live by the proverb "welcome the coming, speed the parting guest," so I do not think I had a tendency to chase after someone who is running away or to want what others have.

Even so, I once had a shocking experience. When I worked at the Nagoya branch office of a Tokyo-based trading house, each day I would walk about two kilometers (a little over one mile) from the office to the company dormitory, where I lived. One day, as I walked down a wide road close to Sakae (downtown district) on my way home, a young female fortune-teller stopped me and said, "Hey, mister. Come over here." I was afraid that she had seen a shadow of death in me or something, so I walked over. Then, she told me, "You won't be able to get married" [*laughs*]. I asked her why, to which she replied, "Because you have no desires." She then went on, "Your aura shows no desires at all, so there is no way you'll be able to get married. You probably wouldn't be able to pursue a woman in order to marry her. Given this, the only way for you to get married will be for the woman to make the decision." She was rather cruel to have told me that. I think she was about the same age as me, but she said, "In your case, the woman will decide for you. You won't make the decision yourself because you have no desires whatsoever. With the attitude, you won't be able to date anyone." I simply said, "Oh, I see."

You may have read a similar story in my collection of poems. Back when the incident occurred, I felt a little offended that a stranger would tell me something like that. I was simply walking two kilometers to the dormitory to save money instead of taking a cab or the train, but was suddenly called over [*making hand gestures*] only to be told that I would not be able to get married because I did not have the desire in my aura. According to what she said, people usually emit an aura that shows a desire to "get" someone. Apparently, most men walk along the street looking at the women and thinking, "If there is a good one around, I'm going to date her." I clearly remember her telling me, "You have no aura of that kind, so you won't be able to get married."

I guess some people can tell. As a matter of fact, in my first marriage, perhaps I was "hunted down" [*laughs*]. I was the one "captured with a harpoon," not the one trying to find a marriage partner. I was much like a whale captured with a harpoon and taken away. But I did have my own "poison" like a Japanese puffer fish. "Please go ahead if you would like to try puffer fish." That was my attitude. A puffer fish is delicious, but it may be a bit dangerous to eat because it is not the type of fish you can eat with a simple way of cooking. Since I knew I possessed a "lethal poison," I did not go out and encourage people to "have a bite of me." I did not stop women who wanted to get to know me, but I did come with "poison." So, women were probably in a dilemma, caught between their desire to "eat the puffer fish" and their desire to save themselves. Of course, I am telling you this half in jest.

Seeking love from others is like seeking water in a desert

Many people in the world lament not being able to find happiness, but my advice to them is to change their mindset. The desire to take from others to satisfy yourself is like looking for water in a desert; your thirst will never be quenched.

For instance, some men dump women the moment they succeed in "hunting" them. Women should stay away from these kinds of men. They chase after women as long as the women are trying to get away from them, are rejecting them, or are reluctant to go out with them. But as soon as the women give into the men's advances and agree to marry them, the men immediately try to dump their lovers. They are the type to think, "I'm no longer interested in someone I've already caught. I'm not going to feed a fish I've already caught." They release the fish they caught as soon as they catch another fish. Such men do exist, so women should be wary; they will never be happy with these types of men. Women who marry men like that simply cannot be happy.

The one doing the chasing will never be satisfied because they are like a traveler who is always thirsty; drinking seawater will never satisfy their thirst. This is what the Bible says. Even if you drink the abundant seawater in front of you, it will not quench your thirst but will only make it worse, so it is best not to drink it at all. This is true. Some people believe they are making progress by increasing their desires more and more, but unfortunately, they are not making any progress at all.

5

Overcome the Self-Centered Way and Become Truly Successful

The hidden efforts of top celebrities

Some people achieve their goals through academic studies while others become successful in arts and entertainment. In a book I read recently, it talked about how popular artists are 90 percent made through hard work and effort. It said that people tend to believe that artists are successful because of their talent or that their agencies only recruit people with talent, but actually, those who have made a name for themselves are all hard workers.

I used to know a man who believed he could become an actor. He boasted that he resembled the actor Takuya Kimura and claimed that he could and did teach him. Sorry for going off on a tangent, but anyway, according to the book, Kimura has never brought a script with him to a film studio, which means that he memorizes the whole of each script before coming to work. He puts in the effort to memorize each script completely. Average actors would probably bring the script with them and memorize or practice their lines before going on the set, but apparently, Kimura did not bring the script because he memorized the whole thing.

The book also said that the actor Junichi Okada has made it a habit to read one book and watch three movies every day since his high school years. This is not an easy routine to practice. If you watch three movies after reading a book, your brain will be fried toward the end. Perhaps he watched the third movie with brain fog. Apparently, this habit of his often worried his mother, but he made such a consistent effort. Okada is also certified as a master of three different kinds of martial arts that use sword-like weapons.

The book described how successful artists are all hard workers, which is not surprising. There are many people with talent. But even if you gather many people like that, only those who make efforts behind the scenes and earn a good reputation among the people around them will survive. People like this tend to have longer careers. It takes effort to earn a good reputation. It means making efforts when others are not looking. It also means not being full of yourself. These are important points.

I once saw a quiz show on TV that featured students from the University of Tokyo. The guest that day was the Japanese actress Suzu Hirose. When the host, who is a comedian, asked the students, "Do you know who she is?" some of them didn't know of her. So, he introduced her to them. Then, the students commented that she must be living an easy life with her current work. This shocked me because these students had no idea that it is more difficult to be a successful actress like Suzu Hirose than it is to enroll in the University of Tokyo. They probably thought that she was not a big deal because they did not know who she was.

Becoming a top star in the world of entertainment is much harder than getting into the University of Tokyo. Stars who make it to the top outcompete tens of thousands, hundreds of thousands, or even millions of people, so they should not be underestimated. They are judged on all aspects of their ability. Their entire character is assessed, so just having good looks is not enough to make them popular for a long time.

There is an actress who is said to be the rebirth of the ninth-century *waka* poet Ono-no-Komachi who was renowned for her beauty. Apparently, this actress failed all 100 auditions she applied for. This was partly because she was attending Meiji University back then and only had free time to prepare for them during summer, winter, and spring breaks. Even so, the fact that she failed all 100 auditions means there must be plenty of beautiful people other than her. She was later chosen as the person with the most beautiful face wanted by young Japanese women. Given that even someone with her looks failed so many auditions, you must be able to find many similarly beautiful faces among the people auditioning.

Thus, it is not at all easy to stand out in a crowd of talented people. Competition in the field of entertainment is more intense than simply competing to excel in studies or to get into a good company. It is extremely tough to survive while being continuously under the scrutiny of the public. There are people who draw attention in their first year and then disappear in their second or third year. This is actually quite common. Those who remain in the spotlight for years make efforts beyond the level of an individual; they make systematic efforts that are similar to the efforts needed to run corporations. Without this, it is almost impossible to survive in the world of entertainment over a span of 10, 20, or 30 years. This is something we must keep in mind.

Long-term achievers versus one-hit wonders

Some people are talented, good-looking, well-educated, employed at a reputable company or public office, or graduates of a renowned university. But this simply means they passed the first round of qualifiers when it comes to society. After that, they need to win against tens of thousands of others to walk the road to success.

A good, recent example is Pikotaro, who became so famous that even the U.S. president's granddaughter could imitate him (at the time of the lecture). When former Japanese Prime Minister Shinzo Abe visited U.S. President Donald Trump, he apparently saw Trump's granddaughter dancing like Pikotaro. However, in his second year, Pikotaro had no hit songs, and by his third year, he barely appeared on TV. Something can become popular without any particular reason. But sadly, one-hit wonders do not last.

So, having talent alone is not enough. Something may become a hit thanks to timing or luck, but the question will be whether it is a fleeting success or becomes a lasting one. This is an extremely important point. People such as business owners who continue to develop their companies or actors and actresses who have been popular from a young age all possess a quality that enables them to achieve long-term success. There are actors who are popular well into their 50s. The Japanese actress Kirin Kiki, for example, still appears in popular TV programs and dramas even at 75 years of age (at the time of the lecture).

Successful writers continue to publish books even after producing a best-selling book or receiving a literary award such as the Naoki Prize or the Akutagawa Prize. These people always have something they can keep working on. We need to recognize this point well. Their accomplishments are not solely due to their innate talents; they did not just happen to dig up some diamonds or lumps of gold.

The same is true of singers who have become successful as a result of being chosen in talent shows like the old "Star Tanjo!" (literally, "A Star Is Born!"). I remember that the show had its contestants sing cover songs and those who won five to ten times were selected to become professional singers. But if you become a professional singer this way, it is extremely difficult to sing your own songs and keep producing new hit songs. Please keep this in mind.

Self-centered people are unable to keep going. They can make efforts to hone their skills or work hard to pass an exam for a short time because, by doing so, they can gain more recognition or receive praise from others. They can make short-term efforts and if they are talented enough, they will be able to succeed. However, they need to know that, in the end, they won't be able to win against someone who has continued to make efforts tirelessly even after attaining success.

The reason why late bloomers tend to last

The same tendency can be observed in company management. According to Peter Drucker, people who are highly regarded as young recruits rarely remain as top-level candidates for CEO in their 30s. Many of them do not make it to that level. Instead, people who barely stand out in the beginning tend to become high-potential candidates by the time they are 30. From this perspective, Drucker says, the American MBA system, where new graduates who attend graduate school for two years to obtain an MBA degree are immediately hired as the vice president of a company and receive special treatment, has become the source of company failure in America.

The Japanese company system is better in this sense because all employees, regardless of whether they are white-collar or blue-collar, can hope to attain success as they continue working at the same company for many years. At Toyota, an employee initially hired as a factory worker could be promoted to become the factory manager or an even higher position. This is a better system because the course of a person's working life cannot be determined in such a short time span. This is what Drucker says, which is probably based on statistical analysis or an analysis of many different companies.

When people find themselves in the limelight at an early stage, they tend to grow arrogant and become preoccupied with how to make themselves look good. On the other hand, people who attract attention slowly, that is, the "late bloomers," have enough time to build themselves up or train themselves. The long period of perseverance they undergo gives them the power to be resilient. That is why people who become successful in their later years often tend to remain active for a long time after achieving success.

Now that I think about it, I should not call myself a late bloomer because I demonstrated my abilities relatively early. However, I did not become conceited. My children often argued with me and asked me, "Why didn't you stand up as a religious leader and launch religious activities right after you opened your spiritual channel and started receiving messages from the spirits in heaven?" They probably thought that taking action right away is the smart thing to do and that remaining in obscurity for six years like I did is nonsensical.

But I believe I had more common sense about this. I was not conceited enough to believe that, because I could receive spiritual messages from great high spirits of the past when I was still in my early 20s, I could quickly accept that I was Buddha, as they told me. I knew I still needed to make efforts of my own. The high spirits who gave me spiritual messages were historical figures who had left behind great legacies in this world, so I needed to be an equally outstanding person who was worthy of their attention. Considering the Law of the Same Wavelengths, it would normally be impossible to receive spiritual messages from high spirits like them. Indeed, I was extremely prudent. Over a few years, I kept verifying the authenticity of their messages and confirming that these high spirits really were who they said they were. At the same time, I continued to make efforts to train and polish myself. So, I never became conceited.

Make continuous efforts to achieve long-lasting success

This morning, I was listening to a lecture I gave 30 years ago, in 1989, titled, "Love, Nurture, and Forgive" while reading a book. (The lecture is compiled in *The Way to Human Perfection: Best Selection of Ryuho Okawa's Early Lectures Vol. 2* [New York: IRH Press, 2024].) When my secretary came into my study and poured some coffee for me, I told her, "You know, this is a lecture from 30 years ago, but 'this guy' is pretty good. He is lecturing well. He might be better than the current me." She replied, "Well, I don't know about that" [*laughs*].

I was surprised to hear myself speaking so eloquently for an hour as if I were speaking from a manuscript I had memorized, considering the lecture was given 30 years ago, in 1989. Now, I am confident enough to look back at it and say that it is not bad, but back then I was desperate. I gave my all in every lecture and I had no idea whether my lectures were good or bad. But my audience gradually grew, so it confirmed that the number of repeaters and newcomers, who came after hearing a good reputation, was growing. Because of that, I did not feel that I was failing. At the same time, however, I was aware that I could lose my popularity at any time, much like the example I just gave about Pikotaro.

There used to be a Japanese religious leader named Shinji Takahashi, who led a group called GLA and passed away about 10 years before I started Happy Science. Now, he is barely recognized by the public and is gradually being forgotten. One of our Happy Science executives has a mother-in-law who once worked closely with Takahashi through GLA's women's section and knew him very well. According to her, Takahashi's younger sister would say that her brother had been saying the same thing for the entire year. Toward the end of his activities, he always said the same thing. He just repeated the same thing. She said something like that, so I was curious, and I listened to his lectures on tape and heard him repeatedly saying things like, "I know things without studying them. I know everything through inspiration." I thought that this must be the very reason why he was repeating the same thing.

I also heard from someone else who had been to Takahashi's house that, since he lived in a small, ordinary house, no one was jealous of him and he was well-received by his followers. Apparently, it was the type of house that you could drop by to have dinner. When I asked about Takahashi's collection of books, the person said, "He had two bookcases, but only had about two shelves of religious books. The rest were filled with books about electrical engineering, which he needed for his business." After I heard that Takahashi only owned two shelves worth of religious books, I could easily identify the books he must have sourced from when giving his lectures.

This example shows that even religious leaders can run out of things to say and end up repeating the same thing over and over again if they do not keep studying. It may work for them to talk about the same thing if they give a talk in a new place and to a new audience, but it will gradually become harder to attract an audience, unlike a *rakugo* comedian who can keep attracting people with the same skit. What is more, if a religious leader can only talk about the same thing each time, it will be very difficult for them to manage their group in an organized way.

It is certainly a good thing to have outstanding abilities that enable you to attain success rather quickly. But unfortunately, people who can only sell themselves by talking badly about others and bragging about how much better they are do not fulfill the conditions to achieve further success. The same is true for those who constantly blame their failures on their upbringing. Success requires an element of continuity, and to continue succeeding, you need to keep making efforts. Without continuous efforts, it will be difficult to attain long-lasting success. You must not lead a disorderly life, either. It is extremely important to maintain a well-disciplined lifestyle and to do what you should do properly and consistently. You must also be mindful of your mental and physical health.

6

Clearing Away the Desire for Self-Protection Is the Starting Point of Enlightenment

The self-centered way leads you to be conceited and a fall from grace

I have talked about why it is a problem to live a self-centered life. To put it simply using a different expression, it is problematic because you will become conceited like a *tengu* (long-nosed goblin). The word "tengu" does not simply refer to an abstract idea but to a real spiritual existence. In the other world, tengus do exist, and you can end up becoming one if you live in a self-centered way.

Many beings who appear as tengus in ancient Japanese religions claim that they are gods, but in truth, they lack wisdom. This is because they are always seeking praise and admiration. When people always want to be praised or admired by others, they tend to be careless and will end up falling from grace. And they repeatedly fall from grace. I am impressed by the ancient Japanese people who discovered this tendency of tengu. Tengu-type people display a similar pattern of behavior. There is a Japanese proverb that says, "Self-conceit is the death of art (You stop growing once you become conceited)," and this is, indeed, true. Humility is important, not because you will be praised for it, but because you will not grow further unless you are humble. This is an essential point.

True rock and roll is a liberation movement

Taking music as an example, some people think that rock and roll goes against social norms and the values of parents or schoolteachers. However, if you can create rock music at the level of The Beatles or John Lennon, you will gain the power to enthrall hundreds of millions of people around the world and generate tremendous profits. The Beatles were an immense success even as a business, so just because they played rock music did not mean that they were merely going against social standards; to the contrary, they walked the royal road like "kings."

In the 1970s and 1980s, John Lennon could not hold concerts in China, the Soviet Union, or Eastern Europe. He recorded a song that criticized Mao Zedong. Although he wanted to put it on the A-side of the vinyl record, it ended up being put on the B-side because of various concerns about how it would be received. The Beatles were banned in post-war communist countries, so they could not sing or share their songs there. From this, it is obvious that their activities did not simply contain an anti-social element but also an anti-totalitarian spirit. Their underlying motivation was to launch a movement to spread freedom and love among people. This is precisely why John Lennon returned to a high dimension in heaven (refer to *The Laws Of Messiah* [New York: IRH Press, 2022] and *John Lennon's Message from Heaven* [Tokyo: HS Press, 2020]).

Therefore, it is wrong to consider rock as merely a form of rebellion. There is both rock music that challenges the values prevailing in society that go against God's Will, as well as rock that corrupts the times. I believe we need to look at the true nature of rock music from a broader perspective.

I, myself, grew up well-behaved. Even after entering the workforce, I was a rather hardworking, role-model-type employee. After launching Happy Science, too, I more or less adopted an orthodox style of work and management. But the work I have been doing is intended to destroy everything on Earth that goes against the Will of God. I have continuously destroyed things that went against God's Will and kept fighting to prevent the forces of hell from expanding and engulfing the entire world. That is why I am happy when people tell me that my work or the Happy Science movies are like "rock." For instance, our actors have commented that the movie, *Immortal Hero* (Executive Producer and Original Story by Ryuho Okawa, released in 2019), was rock-like in

2019 and that it would continue to be like rock even 3,000 or 4,000 years later.

I hope people will understand the zeal behind my work. So, "rock" is not just a word that is used to describe a delinquent person. It is a movement to liberate the people who have become enslaved by the mistaken common sense of this world. I would be grateful if you could understand this.

Other-Power will come down to you as you make efforts every day

In this chapter, I have talked about why it is a problem to live a self-centered life. I do not think I have spoken enough about it, but I have tried to give you an orthodox explanation. I believe there are points I must make again and again.

So why is it a problem to live based on the desire to protect yourself, which I mentioned in the beginning? The answer has to do with the starting point of my own enlightenment. If you only think about yourself and constantly blame others and the environment, or accuse those around you, a "cloud" will form like smog. The cloud will form around your spirit body and block the light of your guardian and guiding spirits from pouring into you. It then leads you to be connected to the spirits in hell. If you constantly speak ill of others, the

Asura spirits or even more atrocious spirits will come to possess you. There are all kinds of spirits in hell, such as Asura spirits, spirits of lust, and ogres, who will all come to possess you. But you are the one who produced the cloud to attract them. It is an "exhaust gas" that is produced by your desire for self-protection, so you must clear it away yourself.

When I understood this, I realized that people need to stop producing the gas and wipe their clouded "windows" or "mirrors" so they become crystal clear. Unless they do this, the light of heaven will not shine down on them. I realized that the light of the high spirits only comes down when people's minds are clear.

Some people at Happy Science can channel spirits, but they need to keep what I have just said in mind. This is the starting point of enlightenment, but you need to keep it in mind until the end, because if you forget about it, you will stray from the right path and derail yourself. If you derail yourself, it will be very difficult to get back on the right track.

So, every day, examine carefully whether you have produced any poisonous exhaust gas and if you did, remove it yourself as much as you can. This kind of Self-Power and the practice of self-reflection are needed. Other-Power will come down to those who do this every day. I hope you will understand this deeply.

CHAPTER FOUR

The Challenge to Establishing the Imperishable Truth

—Polish Your Mind Fully and Illuminate the World

Recorded in Japanese on March 17, 2012
at Happy Science Holy Land Shikoku Shoshinkan in Tokushima, Japan.
English translation.

1

I Want to Leave Behind an Imperishable Truth that Lasts for Thousands of Years

In the near future, the people of the world will choose Tokushima as the "New Mecca"

I arrived in Tokushima yesterday and visited the expected site of the Holy Land El Cantare Seitankan (later opened in 2016) in Kawashima Town. We are planning to build a seminar hall, or a place of worship, that will fit about 1,000 people, so I am excited to see how Happy Science will continue to grow in the coming decades. I can see many people visiting Tokushima from all over the world. I also anticipate that international flights will soon be able to land directly in Tokushima, although I am not sure whether the airport will still be called Awaodori Airport or will be changed to El Cantare Airport by then.

Kawashima Special Temple seems to be developing further, too. I am happy to see that we are making progress, little by little, every time I visit Tokushima. I hear that local branches are opening even in towns I have never heard of, nationwide and overseas, which makes me happy but does not tell me how much progress we are making. But whenever I come back to my hometown and compare the current state of Happy Science to what it used to be, I can see a big difference in the level of development. So, I can confirm that we are surely making progress.

Every time I return to Kawashima Town, it feels like there are fewer houses and fewer people, but now that I think about it, maybe it's just that it appeared to me to be a bustling town when I was younger. Because Happy Science is becoming more and more sophisticated, you may be having a hard time adapting to it.

By the way, on the way here today, I saw a poster of our movie that is set in Shibuya, Tokyo, posted on the billboard next to the Kawashima Special Temple. It did look flashy, urbane, and certainly out of place. I worried for a second whether people living in the countryside would even be interested in watching a movie like that. It gives the impression that Japan is just the area around Shibuya, so perhaps people think our religion is a little flashy. That may make it hard for you to carry out missionary activities every day. But now that we are entering the stage of spreading the Truth to the masses, I hope I will be able to give lectures that reach even more people.

We have a few more days until the Commemoration of the Day of Great Enlightenment (March 23). We should especially rejoice in the fact that Shikoku, of all places in Japan, was chosen this time as the place of most significance (being my birthplace in this life). I am also happy that this land of Tokushima will soon be known to people around the world and will be loved by many. As an article in the Happy Science monthly magazine says, our missionary activities have been carried out so far and wide that, in Nepal, one in two people already knows my name. Apparently, they think that I "fled" to Japan this time* [*laughs*]. Anyway, I believe that, in the near future, people from around the world will choose Tokushima as the "New Mecca" and will make their pilgrimage here. So, I would be grateful if you could make this town prosper further and develop greater capacity to accept them.

The times and people will change, but the imperishable Truth will continue to exist

Let me first summarize my main message for today. Today's title, "The Challenge to Establishing the Imperishable Truth," is related to the main book of this year (2012), *Secrets of the Everlasting Truths* (New York: IRH Press, 2012). We are aiming to achieve something that will not go out of fashion after having short-term success. In the current age, many things come and go in a short cycle, including businesses and artists in the entertainment industry. Things become famous suddenly and then quickly die out. However, we are not aiming to achieve fleeting success. I always keep in mind that we must create values that will remain for thousands of years into the future, and I always think about giving lectures that will be left behind for the people of future generations.

After all, what is it that is imperishable? Of course, land and buildings will last for a certain amount of time if you keep fixing them up and preserving them. However, what is ultimately imperishable is the Truth. Especially, if I can leave behind the Truth about the way of the human mind or the laws of the mind, I believe it will be passed on through the generations as something that is imperishable.

Now that 2,500 and 2,000 years have passed since Buddha and Jesus Christ passed away, respectively, people have lost sight of the true thoughts of Buddha and Christ and what they really wanted to teach. This is the current situation. It is harder to learn and master the real Truth if people are not born at the time when the original teachings are taught. So, I am determined to leave behind my teachings in an easy-to-understand way later generations will also be able to learn. Times will change, and so will people's appearances, races, and ethnicities, but the imperishable Truth will continue to exist throughout the ages. I would like to teach all people that such Truth does exist.

I felt this to be true, especially last year, when I traveled around several Asian countries on my Asia Mission Tour. There, I became strongly convinced that my teachings are universal. In a way, I felt that many people around the world understand my teachings more than Japanese people do (refer to *The Real Buddha and New Hope* and *Love and Spiritual Power* [Tokyo: Happy Science, 2021 and 2024]). For example, in Japan, it would be hard to believe that 90 percent of an audience of 10,000 people would become new members of Happy Science after just listening to a 30-minute lecture. Japanese people would be very cautious and say, "I will think about membership after reading and studying more of your books." On the other hand, people overseas join Happy Science one after another after just listening to a 30-minute lecture of mine. This shows that my words are reaching their hearts, or that my thoughts speak to them. It was the very guidance they've been waiting for. They feel my lectures strike them at the core and resonate in their hearts. This also means that Japan is distant from religion in its current state. I want to break through this situation and make religion regain the position it truly deserves.

A silent revolution has been taking place around the world

I have published many books, some of which contain specialized knowledge, so it is possible that you may find them difficult to read. Depending on your personal preference, some books feel more difficult to read while others may be easier to understand. But I am trying to "toss the ball" in all kinds of directions so that even people who are not religiously inclined have the chance to connect with God. These books, which include spiritual messages, are starting to affect Japanese politics, diplomacy, and the economy, as well as other countries. This has never happened before. People are sensitive to our spiritual messages and are starting to react based on them, so we can say that, unexpectedly, a revolution has silently been taking place simultaneously around the world. It is, indeed, a silent revolution.

Of course, even though the concept of the rebirth of Buddha has been accepted in countries like India, Sri Lanka, and Nepal, it does not necessarily mean that their regimes will go through significant change. However, for materialistic countries like China, which is Japan's neighbor, acknowledging the rebirth of Buddha could trigger a complete change in their regime. This is something they fear. Their regime could be completely overthrown without a single weapon or bullet, meaning they would revert from being an atheist or materialistic country back into a country that believes in God or Buddha. China seems to be sensing this threat. North Korea also seems to fear us because we published a "terrifying" book for them called *Kita-chosen owari no hajimari* (lit. "North Korea—The Beginning of the End"). We are fighting against nuclear missiles with our words. Words are that powerful in this modern age. We are now demonstrating how much power words have by translating my books and publishing them worldwide.

A savior always uses True Words to fight. Fighting against the darkness or ignorance of the earthly world with True Words is the work of a savior. Sometimes, people who compete with or oppose the savior may appear, or what appears to be darkness may rise, but I hope you will know that they, too, are simply part of the drama that should be passed down to future generations. True Words will not be handed down properly into the future without some form of exciting drama. True Words delivered in a lecture are never accepted and understood without any trouble. There is always some drama that comes with them, often manifesting as ordeals and difficulties. But they also make me feel how valuable my work is.

I am shaking up Japan as the national teacher. I am also sending out various pieces of information to other countries as the world teacher. I am becoming a very unique kind of existence now. Today, I am sending out light from Tokushima to the world. I intend to follow my fate and go as far as I can. I truly wish from the bottom of my heart that you, too, will become even stronger, nurture the younger generations, and develop Happy Science twofold, threefold, and even further.

2

Aim to Return to Heaven by Learning to Control Your Mind

Use your power to row along "the river of fate"

I have used the term "Imperishable Truth," but what does it mean? What are we aiming for? Let me explain it to you since I am here.

Happy Science teaches that, basically, everyone can control their own mind. Of course, we are largely affected by environmental factors and the people around us, but I always teach that you must not simply be blown to and fro by them. Instead of being blown around by the times, the environment, or the people around you, you must use your power to control your own mind and row along "the river of fate." I have taught various ways of doing this.

Let me put it even more simply. In a nutshell, I am teaching you how to control your mind so that you will not fall into hell and instead return to heaven after living decades of life in this world. I want you to master this method. This is the basic teaching that you must learn at a minimum. Those who have studied at Happy Science and attained an entry-level of enlightenment shall not end up in hell after death. At the very least, they will not go there. Even if a natural disaster, an outbreak of war, an economic crisis, an incurable disease, financial difficulties, or a fatal accident forces them to suddenly leave this world, as long as they have attained the minimum level of enlightenment as Happy Science believers, they will surely return to heaven without getting lost. This is the baseline that we must strive to achieve.

It is estimated that nearly 20,000 people died from the 2011 Great East Japan Earthquake. I have heard that there were Happy Science believers among them. However, I do not think that any of their souls are wandering on earth as lost spirits. Happy Science is now the number one religion in Japan in terms of its power of salvation. Unlike the old religions that have become empty vessels, Happy Science has real power to actually save people's souls. We have "living teachings" that are taught in modern language. So, even if the people who are studying the Truth at Happy Science were to suddenly lose their lives in a tsunami or an earthquake, their souls will by no means be lost or fall into hell. This is our fundamental stance. There is no mistake about this.

The thoughts that are creating hell in your mind

• Anxiety

Then, how can you cultivate a mind that allows you to return to heaven? Or, to put it even more simply, "What kinds of thoughts are creating hell in your mind?"

One is, of course, anxiety. These are the worries you have in your daily life, worries about life in general, and worries about the future. The battle against anxiety, or overcoming worries, is one of the challenges you need to tackle.

• Fear

Another one is fear. How will you fight against fear? Various worries will develop into fear, which will loom over you. You will experience this kind of fear in your life.

Death is probably the greatest fear for people who are living a materialistic, worldly life. The death of their family members and their own death will scare them the most. The question is whether you can overcome this fear. If you truly believe in the Happy Science teachings, you should be able to overcome this fear. You can overcome your fears as well as your anxieties.

• Dissatisfaction

A smaller element is the battle against dissatisfaction. You probably experience dissatisfaction in many ways as you live in this world. You may feel discontent when things do not go the way you want them to or when everything goes against your wishes. As you fight against this and express discontent in your attitude, you may end up creating hellish thoughts in your mind. The battle against dissatisfaction is another challenge you need to tackle.

In this world, it is almost impossible to fulfill all your desires, so you will certainly develop a sense of dissatisfaction in some way. It is inevitable. When this happens, you need to think about what the Imperishable Truth is. You may be feeling discontent from the perspective of your physical self, but if you ask yourself how much it really means to you, you will realize that the things in this world will all eventually pass, so you should not concern yourself with them. Whether you are living in Naruto City or Tokushima City, for example, does not make much difference from the perspective of heaven. Some of you may be dissatisfied about not being able to afford to live in Tokushima City, but you should not let it be the reason you fall into hell. If you did, it would be your fault for being dissatisfied over such a trifling matter. Instead, you can just think, "I can enjoy the beautiful scenery of the ocean (in Naruto City) every day." You may prefer living in a lively place with more cars, but there are different ways to look at it. You should not think in a way that creates a hellish area in your mind.

3

The True Way to See People

Thinking about the words of Bertrand Russell

In relation to dissatisfaction, there is also envy, or jealousy. Envy is deep-rooted and is another element that drags your mind down into hell.

This morning, I happened to read a passage from the book, *The Conquest of Happiness*, by the philosopher Bertrand Russell. In the book, he clearly wrote, "Envy is the basis of democracy," which I was taken aback by. I am not as blunt or straightforward as he was. I suppose he could say that because, after all, he was a mathematician. He bluntly stated that envy is the basis of democracy. Someone with a literary background would use a softer expression like "Envy can become a driving force of democracy." But since Russell had a mathematical mind, he was rather blunt. I was shocked by his straightforwardness.

Democracy can be seen as something wonderful if it is based on the premise that humans are equal because they all have Buddha-nature within them and are all given free will. This is the main reason Happy Science affirms democracy. If democracy is seen in this light, it will be wonderful in that people can attain progress and prosperity using their free will.

However, if you view democracy as a means to produce equality of results and say, "Everyone must be equal. Ultimately, each person's salary, status, lifespan, and everything else must all be the same," then it becomes exactly the same as communism. It will be a "communist democracy." Democracy can be interpreted both ways.

Of course, it does not feel good to see a huge disparity between people. If you compare yourself to others, it can be difficult not to create hell in your mind, even if you are told not to. However, it is impossible to make every aspect of this world equal for everyone. Disparity is inevitable. You can see this if you take a look at other people—some of them passionately work, study, or play sports, while others do not. Some people are born beautiful, while others, unfortunately, are not. But even if they are not born beautiful, they may make efforts to be able to stand and speak in front of others [*pointing at himself with his right hand*] [*audience laughs*]. I actually feel embarrassed to see many of my old photo albums being displayed here in the Holy Land Shikoku Shoshinkan (at the time of the lecture). But since there is no way to retouch the photos, there is nothing I can do about it.

As you can see, the idea of equal results is impossible to realize in reality. Although you may be able to adjust the results to fit within a certain range so that they all appear to be similar, they will never truly be the same. To give you an example, there will be people who become a CEO and those who will not. Not everyone can become a CEO. If every company was just run by a CEO and there were no other employees, you could probably say that everyone can be a CEO. But companies are made up of a multitude of people, so it is impossible for everyone to be the CEO, no matter how hard you may insist that they can. Things do not work out well when everyone wants to be a leader.

Therefore, Russell may have a point in saying that the desire to seek equal results that comes from envy is the basis of democracy.

Humans are all connected to the Great Tree of Life

I believe that Buddha's Truth helps people transcend and overcome envy, which is a negative aspect of democracy. Some people believe that each person is an independent individual who is totally unconnected. These people only strive to achieve their own self-realization and happiness and do not care about others. Their thinking is based on the idea that everyone should mind their own business and seek their own happiness. These people live in a world that is not that different from a world of wild animals. If you study the Truth, however, the way you think will change, and you will realize that everyone is a child of God who is connected to the Great Tree of Life called God. Once you know that all souls branched off from this parent soul and that everyone is interconnected, you will understand that Jesus taught to love your neighbor because the act of loving other people is the same as loving yourself. In other words, you and others are not separate but are one and the same; we are all connected to the Great Tree of Life.

We need to reconsider envy from this perspective. If you strongly believe in individualism or separatism and become envious, it will form a hell that you cannot be saved from. It is a matter of how you look at other people. You should think of all people as children of Buddha or God and know that they are all connected to the great, one and only God. Each person is working hard, making creative efforts, and striving to achieve progress and prosperity to realize God's prosperity on earth. If you adopt these views, you will be able to overcome the notion that democracy is based on envy. The "one person, one vote" system indeed brings about equality, but in this system, people will be envious if someone has more than one vote. However, when you think that everyone is born to fulfill their own unique role, you can acquire a different perspective.

4

Polish Your Mind Neatly and Illuminate the World

Your mindset changes the moment you wish to celebrate others

Once you gain the perspective I have just described, you will be able to celebrate people who have made efforts, achieved success, or are taking on extremely meaningful work in this world. As I have been saying continuously since the early stages of Happy Science's activities, your mindset changes the moment you wish to celebrate others.

What will happen if you just want to win against others or stand above them? What will happen if you are frustrated when you lose to others? People tend to feel this way in this earthly world. This tendency is often observed in moneymaking businesses and in the stock and securities markets. It can also be seen in school entrance examinations and what they entail. The need to compete and rise above others will continue as you grow older. But you need to remember that these kinds of competitive systems are meant to exist as a way to encourage each person to polish their soul, so you should not think that life is all about competition. I am saying that you should have a wish to celebrate others.

Looking back at my life, it may appear as if I succeeded rather smoothly. I was born and raised in Kawashima Town, went to a school in Tokushima City, then moved to Tokyo, and even worked in New York City. From a subjective point of view, however, I went through many different types of suffering, setbacks, and failures before reaching adulthood. To be honest, there was a time when I felt envious of the people who were born into a fortunate environment or were born with natural intelligence. But when I realized that I should want to celebrate others, I felt that my competition with other people ended for the first time.

Once this happened, I only had myself to compete against. Conquering yourself is your real mission. Your mission in life is to win against yourself and let your God-given talent bloom to the fullest extent. So, you must not get in the way of other people who are also seeking to fulfill their mission. All you need to do is focus on your own mission. Fulfilling your mission is the most important work for you to do.

As you polish yourself and try to help others, many people will come to support you

I realized that when other people are achieving success, I must make an effort to celebrate them, because doing this will lead me to develop myself as a human being. I awakened to this Truth when I was still around 20 years old. Since then, I have been able to maintain peace of mind while entrusting everything to God. I just needed to focus on polishing myself.

When you focus on polishing yourself, the work you do will gradually expand. You will then be recognized by others and many people will come to support you. On the contrary, if you try to do something expecting other people's support, you will not be able to gain their recognition. Those who do something out of a desire to gain recognition from others—in other words, those who take love from others—will not be able to gain recognition, whereas those who polish themselves and work to help others will receive help from those around them and be given an even more important role. I learned that this is the way the world works.

I also confirmed to myself that society will ultimately judge people correctly. I learned that society does not make mistakes on a large scale or make wrong judgments in the long run, so in this regard, I was able to trust and have confidence in society.

Today, I spoke about "The Challenge to Establishing the Imperishable Truth" and explained in simple words what the Imperishable Truth is. I hope that you, too, will focus on how fully and beautifully you can polish your mind—the Buddha-nature or the diamond within you—and illuminate the world. If you do, everything in this world will surely appear to be shining in your eyes. I pray from the bottom of my heart that you will continue to take on this challenge each and every day.

[Translator's note]
The author, Ryuho Okawa, is the rebirth of Shakyamuni Buddha.

CHAPTER FIVE

Awaken to the Value of Your Mind

—Light the Flame of Love in Each and Every Person

Recorded in Japanese on October 30, 1997
at Happy Science Special Lecture Hall.
English translation.

1
Infinite Value Lies within Each Person's Mind

Today, I would like to talk about the mind.

The world is now in confusion. Neither politics nor the economy is going well, and I see shadows looming over Asia. It seems like people have lost sight of the direction the world should be heading in. There do not seem to be any new ideologies that could lead the world from the 21st century and onward. However, in times like this, we must be careful not to judge happiness or unhappiness, or success or failure, based on what is happening outside of us. I believe it is the essential duty of religion to warn people against this way of judgment.

The 20th century, in particular, was a century of materialism. It was an age where people were heavily reliant on material goods. The development of scientific technology allowed people to make great progress in manufacturing goods, and an abundance of goods made people's lives happier in a sense. To overcome the food crisis, there was also rapid progress in food production with the development of fertilizers and various agricultural machinery. In this sense, material wealth cannot be denied completely.

Even so, the happiness we can see and touch is finite, no matter how much we seek it. Given that, what is it that we can seek infinitely as we live in this finite world? It is the potential of human beings that lies deep down within our minds. Everyone has this "treasure" in their mind. Just as oil, coal, iron ore, gold, silver, and diamonds are buried deep underneath the earth, unlimited potential lies dormant in the mind of each and every person. It does not necessarily manifest in a perceptible way as great success. However, you will surely attain everlasting success in your mind as long as you discover and appreciate this unlimited potential.

2

Seek the Happiness of Loving Others

Convenience and material comfort escalate people's desires and make them unhappy

People are now happier in their daily lives. At the same time, they are feeling unhappier on the inside. The unhappiness they suffer seems to be proportionate to the amount of happiness they have gained. This is probably because the convenience of the modern world has worked to escalate people's desires. They used to be satisfied with just earning their daily bread, but now, they are inclined to seek more extravagance and comfort. Lots of people now aspire to attain greater status, fortune, and fame, and to become the ultimate winners in their competition with others.

In reality, only a few people can reach the top of the social pyramid and become the ultimate winners, which means that many people will fall off the sides. However, the misery of modern Japan can be seen in the fall of people who were thought to be at the top of the pyramid; they are falling down from the pyramid, one after another. We have seen many cases of top politicians, bureaucrats, businesspeople, and other well-respected people in society being heavily criticized on the front page of the newspaper as if they were atrocious criminals from birth. Perhaps these incidents reflect the empty value judgments of today's society. "Many people are suffering at the bottom of the pyramid because they cannot climb to the top. The only way they can feel relief is to see the people at the top fall down to where they are and experience a similar kind of misery." This is how people today may think.

When I think about it, however, I am not quite convinced of the idea that only a handful of people can become happy in this world while the rest remain unhappy. People with this mindset only think of happiness as visible results or fame and think that happiness is something that can be measured by external standards. However, what is important is to understand that true happiness is something that is measured by internal standards, or the standards that exist in our own minds.

A heart of love will become an infinite source of happiness

I am not saying this to simply console people. Those who have never seen what is within their minds, or who have yet to discover their minds, may find my talk abstract and think that it is nothing but a fantasy. For someone who does not realize that coal, oil, diamonds, iron ore, and gold ore are buried underneath the earth, soil is just soil. A person who thinks like that can only think about whether they can grow crops there. In the same way, many people are not aware of what is dormant deep within their own minds. But once you realize the existence of the mind and dig up its real value, your mind will become an infinite source of happiness.

Can people of today genuinely feel
The joy of loving other people?
The moments when you feel this joy
Are extremely rare and precious ones.

Look back over the year.
Did you love other people in some way or another?
Did you feel joy in loving other people?
Can you feel happiness in recalling those moments?
I would like you to think about this.

How was this year?
How much joy did you feel in loving other people?
What about the opposite?
Did you self-reflect on the suffering or pain
That you have caused others?

There must have been many events throughout the year.
Even so,
You may not have had many radiant moments
When your mind shed light.

3

What We Need in an Age of Fear

The opposite of fear is love

In the coming age, we may be faced with even tougher situations. I do not want to give prophecies of misfortune, but I must say that those who only seek outward success are likely to experience a series of severe hardships. On the other hand, those who pursue inward success or a profound, spiritual success will be able to live days of fortune, no matter what hardships unfold before their eyes. An age of misfortune is, in a way, an age of fear and anxiety. The ultimate consequence of an age of fear is war, earthquakes, and other natural disasters.

Then, what is the opposite of fear? I would say it is love.

Because people are unable to protect themselves fully,
They are trembling, quivering, and shaking in fear
As they endure suffering, sadness, and tragedy.
People are overwhelmed with fear.
They are worried about facing financial difficulties,
Anxious about the uncertainty of the future,
And even afraid of not being able to survive.

Only love can save people from fear.
Or you could call it kindness,
The wish to help others,
Or a sincere heart that tells others,
"I love you just the way you are."
In an age of fear,
We need more people who cherish others and say,
"You are wonderful just the way you are.
You are already a child of Buddha or a child of God.
I can see the wonderful, shining part of you."
However,
When more and more people
Only think of protecting themselves
And worry about being harmed by others,
Wars break out between countries.
If not war,
A civil war or other domestic crises will occur.

Hold the torch of love high and continue to light up the darkness

Love is what conquers fear.
Love is the power that unites people.
It is also the power that makes people stronger.

It is the power that guides them to hope.
I truly believe so.
Therefore,
What you must do now is
To hold the torch of love high.
Just as a lighthouse emits a beacon of light,
You must continue to light up the darkness.

The light of each person's candle or torch may be small,
But if thousands, tens of thousands, hundreds of thousands,
Or millions of candles come together,
The darkness in this country and the world
Will gradually be driven into a corner
And the world will become brighter.

You do not need to ask for a special miracle.
The source of miracles lies in
The potential of each and every person's mind.
First,
Each one of you
Must light the flame in your own mind.
You must light the flame of hope in your mind.
You all possess infinite potential and
The power to light the torch of love.
You must feel that

These were planted in you
Out of the profound mercy
Of God and Buddha.

4
Missionary Work Is the Proof of Love

I also want you to teach others,
"You will not become happy
By receiving something from others,
By taking away something from others,
Or through external achievements.
You will not become happy by getting something.
There is a way for you to be happy just the way you are."

Teach the value of the mind
To those who have yet to awaken.
Teach them that the mind is like a gem:
The more you polish your mind,
The evermore brilliantly it will shine.

Just as each one of you possesses
A gem of love in your mind,
Other people also have it.
So,
Please tell them that they have a raw gemstone
Lying dormant within their minds.
Please teach them how to polish it.

Teach them that they, too, are precious people
Who deserve to live in a wonderful world
Without having to deprecate themselves or tremble in fear.
This is the meaning of missionary work.

Missionary work is based on love.
It is based on the wish to make people happy.
It is based on the strong wish
To make this world a beautiful place.
Missionary work is love.
Let us continue to love many people
Next year and onward.
Missionary work is the proof of love.
And I will confidently say that it is the only hope.

For a deeper understanding of
The Challenge to Establishing the Imperishable Truth
see other books below by Ryuho Okawa:

The Laws Of Messiah [New York: IRH Press, 2022]

Secrets of the Everlasting Truths [New York: IRH Press, 2012]

The Way to Human Perfection: Best Selection of Ryuho Okawa's Early Lectures Vol. 2 [New York: IRH Press, 2024]

John Lennon's Message from Heaven [Tokyo: HS Press, 2020]

The following books are only available at Happy Science locations. Please see the contact information on p. 178-179.

Twiceborn [New York: IRH Press, 2020]

The Real Buddha and New Hope [Tokyo: Happy Science, 2021]

Love and Spiritual Power [Tokyo: Happy Science, 2024]

ABOUT THE AUTHOR

Founder and CEO of Happy Science Group.

Ryuho Okawa was born on July 7th, 1956, in Tokushima, Japan. After graduating from the University of Tokyo with a law degree, he joined a Tokyo-based trading company. While working at its New York headquarters, he studied international finance at the Graduate Center of the City University of New York. In 1981, he attained Great Enlightenment and became aware that he is El Cantare with a mission to bring salvation to all humankind.

In 1986, he established Happy Science. It now has members in 186 countries across the world, with more than 700 branches and temples, as well as 10,000 missionary houses around the world.

He has given over 3,500 lectures (of which more than 150 are in English) and published over 3,250 books (of which more than 600 are Spiritual Interview Series), and many are translated into 42 languages. Along with *The Laws of the Sun* and *The Laws of Hell*, many of the books have become best sellers or million sellers. To date, Happy Science has produced 28 movies under his supervision. He has given the original story and concept and is also the Executive Producer. He has also composed music and written lyrics for over 450 pieces.

Moreover, he is the Founder of Happy Science University and Happy Science Academy (Junior and Senior High School), Founder and President of the Happiness Realization Party, Founder and Honorary Headmaster of Happy Science Institute of Government and Management, Founder of IRH Press Co., Ltd., and the Chairperson of NEW STAR PRODUCTION Co., Ltd. and ARI Production Co., Ltd.

BOOKS BY RYUHO OKAWA

Related Books

THE LAWS OF THE SUN

ONE SOURCE, ONE PLANET, ONE PEOPLE

ISBN: 978-1-942125-43-3 • $15.95

Why and how did God create this world? What is a spirit and soul? For what purpose are humans living in this world? How can we find true happiness and meaning in life?

The Laws of the Sun answers life's questions humans have always had throughout history.

In this book, Ryuho Okawa outlines the laws that govern the universe and provides a road map for living one's life with greater purpose and meaning.

The Truth taught in this book will significantly transform your life and allow you to develop love and acceptance toward people of all races and religions.

THE LAWS OF ETERNITY

EL CANTARE UNVEILS THE STRUCTURE OF THE SPIRIT WORLD

ISBN: 978-1-958655-16-0 • $17.95

Where do we come from, and where do we go after death?

The Laws of Eternity answers life's most important questions that we are all confronted with at some point or another.

Author Ryuho Okawa takes us on a journey to the other world, a place where we came from before we were born and return to after death.

Open its pages and discover the eternal mysteries and the ultimate secrets of Earth's spirit group that have been covered by the veil of legends and myths.

SECRETS OF THE EVERLASTING TRUTHS

A NEW PARADIGM FOR LIVING ON EARTH

ISBN: 978-1-937673-10-9 • $14.95

Whether or not we notice them, *miracles are actually occurring around us all the time*. In this book, Master Ryuho Okawa explains the whys and hows of spiritual phenomena. He reveals that everlasting spiritual laws *do exist*, and they shape our world and worlds beyond the one we know. Knowing and believing in these laws will allow us to solve the world's problems and bring our entire planet together. Miracles and spiritual occurrences depend not just on Heaven, but ultimately on the spirituality of each one of us and *the power of our own minds—the power of faith*. When you discover the secrets in this book, your view of yourself and the world will be changed dramatically and forever.

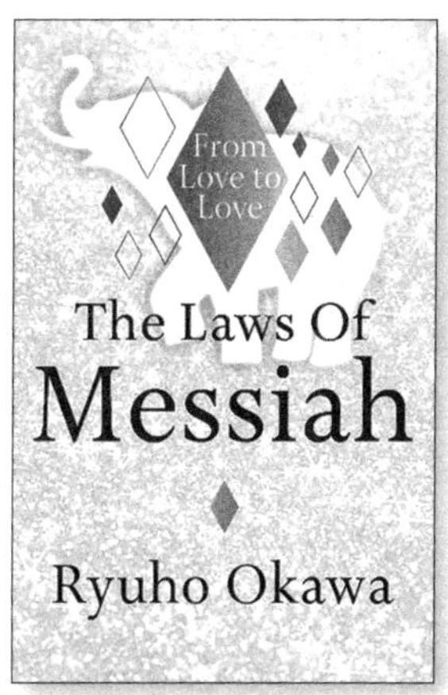

The Laws Of Messiah

From Love to Love

ISBN: 978-1-942125-90-7 • $16.95

"What is Messiah?" This book carries an important message of love and guidance to people living now from the Modern-Day Messiah or the Modern-Day Savior. It also reveals the secret of Shambhala, the spiritual center of Earth, as well as the truth that this spiritual center is currently in danger of perishing and what we can do to protect this sacred place.

Love your Lord God. Know that those who don't know love don't know God. Discover the true love of God and the ideal practice of faith. This book teaches the most important element we must not lose sight of as we go through our soul training on this planet Earth.

What Is Happy Science?

Best Selection of Ryuho Okawa's Early Lectures (Volume 1)

ISBN: 978-1-942125-99-0 • $17.95

The Best Selection series is a collection of Ryuho Okawa's passionate lectures from the ages of 32 to 33 that reveal the mission and goal of Happy Science. Volume 1 teaches the eternal Truth, including the meaning of life, the secret of the mind, the true meaning of love, the mystery of the universe, and how to end hatred and world conflicts.

The Way to Human Perfection

Best Selection of Ryuho Okawa's Early Lectures (Volume 2)

ISBN: 978-1-958655-20-7 • $17.95

The path to enlightenment starts from understanding 'the eternal viewpoint of life.' By recognizing that we have eternal life, we can realize that caring and bringing joy to others are the keys to true happiness and success.

One More Step Forward

The Invincible Thinking to Get You Through Tough Times

ISBN: 978-1-958655-25-2 • $17.95

Success in life is determined not by our circumstances but by our mindset and how we think.

In this book, author Ryuho Okawa reveals from his first-hand experience how the spirit of self-help can create new values.

Okawa is a true self-made man with an indomitable spirit to bring happiness to all humankind. His drive to keep moving forward by taking steady steps through the power of discipline has led to the publication of over 3,200 books in 37 years (at the time of its publication).

Unlock the keys to lifelong growth and success by reading this book.

Be Infinitely Kind

For We Are Living in the Great River of Love

ISBN: 978-1-958655276 • $17.95

What is true love? What is the true definition of kindness? In this book, Ryuho Okawa invites readers to explore the deeper spiritual virtues of love and kindness—essential qualities for building strong, lasting relationships with those we hold dear. Truthfully, the more love we give, the wealthier our souls become.

Kanjizai, Buddha's Omniscient Power of Perception

Going Beyond Time, Space, and the Great Universe

ISBN: 978-1958655290 • $17.95

Kanjizai is a profound spiritual power that allows you to perceive all things. *Kanjizai* unveils what it means to possess real spiritual power—one that inspires humility, sincerity, and the pursuit of genuine enlightenment. *Kanjizai* is a guide to awakening your infinite potential as human being, unveiling the eternal truths of the universe and the Creator.

THE TRUTH ABOUT EARTH, THE UNIVERSE, THE SPIRIT WORLD

LIFE'S Q&A WITH EL CANTARE

ISBN: 978-1-958655-26-9 • $17.95

A compilation of 28 Q&A sessions conducted by author Ryuho Okawa, where he answers numerous intricate questions varying from the theory of evolution to the creation of the multidimensional universe, all without a script.

TRUE BUSHIDO SPOKEN BY AME-NO-MIOYA-GAMI

THE JAPANESE FATHER GOD TEACHES HOW WE SHOULD LIVE AND DIE

ISBN: 978-4823304606 • $20.00

Nearly 30,000 years ago, Ame-no-Mioya-Gami (The Japanese Father God) descended on the foothills of Mt. Fuji in a fleet of spaceships. He taught the values of Justice, Prosperity, Order, and Harmony, which are the original Japanese spirit. In this book, Ame-no-Mioya-Gami speaks on the true meaning behind bushido and why people must regain the samurai spirit.

THE ESSENCE OF BUDDHA

THE PATH TO ENLIGHTENMENT

ISBN: 978-1-942125-06-8 • $14.95

The essence of Shakyamuni Buddha's original teachings of the mind are explained in simple words. Through this book, you will learn how to attain inner happiness, the wisdom to conquer ego, and to enter the path to enlightenment.

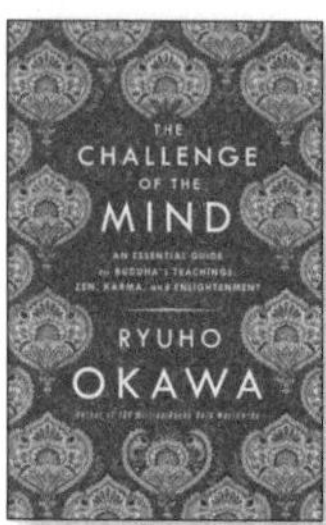

THE CHALLENGE OF THE MIND

AN ESSENTIAL GUIDE TO BUDDHA'S TEACHINGS: ZEN, KARMA AND ENLIGHTENMENT

ISBN: 978-1-942125-45-7 • $16.95

In this book, Ryuho Okawa explains essential Buddhist tenets and how to put them into practice. He offers a solid basis of reason and an intellectual understanding of Buddhist concepts.

THE LAWS OF GREAT ENLIGHTENMENT

ALWAYS WALK WITH BUDDHA

ISBN: 978-1-942125-62-4 • $17.95

Discover the power of forgiveness from Buddha's enlightenment and compassion, and the true relationship of work and enlightenment. In addition, the author reveals his own experience when he attained the Great Enlightenment.

THE ETERNAL BUDDHA

NOW, HERE, IS THE IMPERISHABLE LIGHT

ISBN: 978-1-958655-19-1 • $17.95

Embedded in this book is a message from Eternal Buddha, the parent of your soul. You will discover the true origin of your soul, why you have chosen to be born in this time, and why having faith is important.

THE TEN PRINCIPLES FROM EL CANTARE VOLUME I

RYUHO OKAWA'S FIRST LECTURES ON HIS BASIC TEACHINGS

ISBN: 978-1-942125-85-3 • $16.95

How did Happy Science begin? What are its teachings? What is its aim? This is a compilation of early lectures that built the foundation of Happy Science. The historic moments are captured in this book.

THE TEN PRINCIPLES FROM EL CANTARE VOLUME II

RYUHO OKAWA'S FIRST LECTURES ON HIS WISH TO SAVE THE WORLD

ISBN: 978-1-942125-86-0 • $16.95

Volume II contains passionate messages of Ryuho Okawa filled with the wish to save humankind and build utopia on earth. You can also learn about God's three major inventions, the mission of religion, and more.

WHO IS EL CANTARE?

El Cantare means "the Light of the Earth." He is the Supreme God of the Earth who has been guiding humankind since the beginning of Genesis, and He is the Creator of the universe. He is whom Jesus called Father and Muhammad called Allah, and He is *Ame-no-Mioya-Gami*, the Japanese Father God. He is also known as Vishnu in India and Tiandi in China. Different parts of El Cantare's core consciousness have descended to Earth in the past, once as Alpha and another as Elohim. His branch spirits, such as Shakyamuni Buddha and Hermes, have descended to Earth many times and helped to flourish many civilizations. To build a new civilization on Earth by uniting various religions and integrating various fields of study, a part of the core consciousness has now descended as Master Ryuho Okawa.

Alpha is a part of the core consciousness of El Cantare, who descended to Earth around 330 million years ago. Alpha preached Earth's Truth to harmonize and unify Earth-born humans and space people who came from other planets.

Elohim is a part of the core consciousness of El Cantare, who descended to Earth around 150 million years ago. He gave wisdom, mainly on the differences between light and darkness, good and evil.

Ame-no-Mioya-Gami (The Japanese Father God) is a Being who is close to the core consciousness of Lord El Cantare, and is the Creator God and the Father God who appears in ancient literature, *Hotsuma Tsutae*. It is believed that He descended on the foothills of Mt. Fuji about 30,000 years ago and built the Fuji dynasty, which is the root of the Japanese civilization. Ame-no-Mioya-Gami's Teachings spread to ancient civilizations of other countries in the world.

Shakyamuni Buddha was born in Nepal around 2,600 years ago as the prince of the Shakya clan. When he was 29 years old, he renounced the world and sought enlightenment. He later attained Great Enlightenment and spent most of his life in India teaching and practicing the Truth. He is the founder of Buddhism, which has spread extensively throughout Asia.

Hermes is one of the 12 Olympian gods in Greek mythology, but the spiritual Truth is that he taught the teachings of love and progress around 4,300 years ago, which became the origin of the current Western civilization. He is a hero who truly existed.

Ophealis was born in Greece around 6,500 years ago and was the leader who went on an expedition as far as Egypt. He is the God of miracles, prosperity, and arts, and is known as Osiris in Egyptian mythology.

Rient Arl Croud was born as a king of the ancient Incan Empire around 7,000 years ago and taught about the mysteries of the mind. In the heavenly world, he is responsible for the interactions that take place between Earth and various planets.

Thoth was an almighty leader who built the golden age of the Atlantic civilization around 12,000 years ago. In Egyptian mythology, he is known as God Thoth.

Ra Mu was a leader who built the golden age of the civilization of Mu around 17,000 years ago. As a religious leader and a politician, he ruled by uniting religion and politics.

ABOUT HAPPY SCIENCE

Happy Science is a religious group founded on the faith in El Cantare, who is the God of the Earth and the Creator of the universe. The true essence of human beings is an eternal soul created by God, and we go through the cycle of reincarnation to train and develop our souls. We have been carrying out various activities to spread this spiritual value and build a peaceful and prosperous world that God wishes. At Happy Science, we explore righteousness, in other words, God's Will. This is called the "Exploration of Right Mind." More specifically, it means to practice the Fourfold Path: Love, Wisdom, Self-Reflection, and Progress. This is the path that leads humans to attain happiness that carries over from this world to the next.

Love–practicing "love that gives"
To give love to others without expecting anything in return is the starting point of happiness. By practicing "love that gives," you will become closer to God.

Wisdom—studying spiritual truth
By studying the Truth, you will be able to distinguish good and evil, live righteously, and learn the heart of God. True wisdom leads people to true happiness.

Self-Reflection—correcting your mistakes
Self-reflection is the act of correcting wrongful thoughts and actions you have accumulated during the day and regaining the pure, true nature of the soul.

Progress—creating utopia on earth
True progress is about spreading happiness to others and improving society as you achieve your own success. This will create utopia on earth.

PLACES OF WORSHIP FOR HAPPY SCIENCE

Shoja

—A PLACE TO REFINE YOUR MIND, GAIN SPIRITUAL WISDOM, AND BE REBORN

Happy Science shoja (temple) is a sacred spiritual field where you can deepen your faith and heighten your enlightenment. Under the spiritual guidance of high spirits, shoja holds various seminars to improve individual character and practices ritual prayers to help believers solve their life problems and make progress. By participating in them, you can regain the peaceful and blissful mind that you may have lost in your everyday life.

27 SHOJAS IN JAPAN, 3 SHOJAS OVERSEAS, AND LA DOJO

San Francisco

Local Branch

—A PLACE TO CHANGE YOUR DESTINY

Since 1986, Happy Science has been carrying out various activities to produce people who can truly say, "I am happy." At our local branches, many new believers are being born and are leading better lives through faith in Lord God El Cantare. All kinds of events take place here, such as lecture viewing, book seminars, prayers, and counseling sessions. Everyone is welcome!

HAPPY SCIENCE'S ENGLISH SUTRA

"The True Words Spoken By Buddha"

"The True Words Spoken By Buddha" is an English sutra given directly from the spirit of Shakyamuni Buddha, who is a part of Master Ryuho Okawa's subconscious. The words in this sutra are not of a mere human being but are the words of God or Buddha sent directly from the ninth dimension, which is the highest realm of the Earth's Spirit World.

"The True Words Spoken By Buddha" is an essential sutra for us to connect and live with God or Buddha's Will as our own.

MEMBERSHIPS

MEMBERSHIP

If you would like to know more about Happy Science, please consider becoming a member. Those who pledge to believe in Lord El Cantare and wish to learn more can join us.

When you become a member, you will receive the following sutras: "The True Words Spoken By Buddha," "Prayer to the Lord," and "Prayer to Guardian and Guiding Spirits."

DEVOTEE MEMBER

If you would like to learn the teachings of Happy Science and walk the path of faith, become a Devotee member who pledges devotion to the Three Treasures, which are Buddha, Dharma, and Sangha. Buddha refers to Lord El Cantare, Master Ryuho Okawa. Dharma refers to Master Ryuho Okawa's teachings. Sangha refers to Happy Science. Devoting to the Three Treasures will let your Buddha nature shine, and you will enter the path to attain true freedom of the mind.

Becoming a devotee means you become Buddha's disciple. You will discipline your mind and act to bring happiness to society.

EMAIL OR **PHONE CALL**

Please turn to the contact information page.

ONLINE member.happy-science.org/signup/

CONTACT INFORMATION

Happy Science is a worldwide organization with branches and temples around the globe. For full details, visit happy-science.org. The following are some of our main Happy Science locations:

United States and Canada

New York
79 Franklin St., New York, NY 10013, USA
Phone: 1-212-343-7972
Fax: 1-212-343-7973
Email: ny@happy-science.org
Website: happyscience-usa.org

New Jersey
66 Hudson St., #2R, Hoboken, NJ 07030, USA
Phone: 1-201-313-0127
Email: nj@happy-science.org
Website: happyscience-usa.org

Chicago
33 West Higgins Rd. 4040,
South Barrington, IL 60010, USA
Phone: 1-630-937-3077
Email: chicago@happy-science.org
Website: happyscience-usa.org

Florida
5208 8th St., Zephyrhills, FL 33542, USA
Phone: 1-813-715-0000
Fax: 1-813-715-0010
Email: florida@happy-science.org
Website: happyscience-usa.org

Atlanta
1874 Piedmont Ave., NE Suite 360-C
Atlanta, GA 30324, USA
Phone: 1-404-892-7770
Email: atlanta@happy-science.org
Website: happyscience-usa.org

San Francisco
525 Clinton St.
Redwood City, CA 94062, USA
Phone & Fax: 1-650-363-2777
Email: sf@happy-science.org
Website: happyscience-usa.org

Los Angeles
1590 E. Del Mar Blvd., Pasadena,
CA 91106, USA
Phone: 1-626-395-7775
Fax: 1-626-395-7776
Email: la@happy-science.org
Website: happyscience-usa.org

Orange County
16541 Gothard St. Suite 104
Huntington Beach, CA 92647
Phone: 1-714-659-1501
Email: oc@happy-science.org
Website: happyscience-usa.org

San Diego
7841 Balboa Ave. Suite #202
San Diego, CA 92111, USA
Phone: 1-626-395-7775
Fax: 1-626-395-7776
E-mail: sandiego@happy-science.org
Website: happyscience-usa.org

Hawaii
Phone: 1-808-591-9772
Fax: 1-808-591-9776
Email: hi@happy-science.org
Website: happyscience-usa.org

Kauai
3343 Kanakolu Street, Suite 5
Lihue, HI 96766, USA
Phone: 1-808-822-7007
Fax: 1-808-822-6007
Email: kauai-hi@happy-science.org
Website: happyscience-usa.org

Toronto
845 The Queensway
Etobicoke, ON, M8Z 1N6, Canada
Phone: 1-416-901-3747
Email: toronto@happy-science.org
Website: happy-science.ca

Vancouver
#201-2607 East 49th Avenue,
Vancouver, BC, V5S 1J9, Canada
Phone: 1-604-437-7735
Fax: 1-604-437-7764
Email: vancouver@happy-science.org
Website: happy-science.ca

WORLDWIDE

Tokyo
1-6-7 Togoshi, Shinagawa,
Tokyo, 142-0041, Japan
Phone: 81-3-6384-5770
Fax: 81-3-6384-5776
Email: tokyo@happy-science.org
Website: happy-science.org

London
3 Margaret St.
London, W1W 8RE United Kingdom
Phone: 44-20-7323-9255
Fax: 44-20-7323-9344
Email: eu@happy-science.org
Website: www.happyscience-uk.org

Sydney
516 Pacific Highway, Lane Cove North,
2066 NSW, Australia
Phone: 61-2-9411-2877
Fax: 61-2-9411-2822
Email: sydney@happy-science.org

Sao Paulo
Rua. Domingos de Morais 1154,
Vila Mariana, Sao Paulo SP
CEP 04010-100, Brazil
Phone: 55-11-5088-3800
Email: sp@happy-science.org
Website: happyscience.com.br

Jundiai
Rua Congo, 447, Jd. Bonfiglioli
Jundiai-CEP, 13207-340, Brazil
Phone: 55-11-4587-5952
Email: jundiai@happy-science.org

Seoul
74, Sadang-ro 27-gil,
Dongjak-gu, Seoul, Korea
Phone: 82-2-3478-8777
Fax: 82-2-3478-9777
Email: korea@happy-science.org

Taipei
No. 89, Lane 155, Dunhua N. Road,
Songshan District, Taipei City 105, Taiwan
Phone: 886-2-2719-9377
Fax: 886-2-2719-5570
Email: taiwan@happy-science.org

Taichung
No. 146, Minzu Rd., Central Dist.,
Taichung City 400001, Taiwan
Phone: 886-4-22233777
Email: taichung@happy-science.org

Kuala Lumpur
No 22A, Block 2, Jalil Link Jalan Jalil Jaya
2, Bukit Jalil 57000,
Kuala Lumpur, Malaysia
Phone: 60-3-8998-7877
Fax: 60-3-8998-7977
Email: malaysia@happy-science.org
Website: happyscience.org.my

Kathmandu
Kathmandu Metropolitan City,
Ward No. 15, Ring Road, Kimdol,
Sitapaila Kathmandu, Nepal
Phone: 977-1-537-2931
Email: nepal@happy-science.org

Kampala
Plot 877 Rubaga Road, Kampala
P.O. Box 34130 Kampala, Uganda
Email: uganda@happy-science.org

ABOUT IRH PRESS USA INC.

Founded in 2013, New York-based IRH Press USA Inc. is the North American affiliate of IRH Press Co., Ltd., Japan. The Press exclusively publishes comprehensive titles on Spiritual Truth, religious enrichment, Buddhism, personal growth, and contemporary commentary by Ryuho Okawa, the author of more than 3,250 unique publications, with hundreds of millions of copies sold worldwide. For more information, visit Okawabooks.com.

Follow us on:

- Facebook: Okawa Books
- Instagram: OkawaBooks
- Youtube: Okawa Books
- Twitter: Okawa Books
- Pinterest: Okawa Books
- Goodreads: Ryuho Okawa

NEWSLETTER

To receive book-related news, promotions, and events, please subscribe to our newsletter below.

irhpress.com/pages/subscribe

AUDIO / VISUAL MEDIA

YOUTUBE

PODCAST

Visit the above to learn more about Ryuho Okawa's books. Topics range from self-help, current affairs, spirituality, religion, and the universe.